BOB HOPE

Thanks for the memory

"Laughter is the only tonic I need to keep young. Why go on working? I just love it . . . and so does my tax man!"

BOB HOPE, 1987

"Bob Hope has been a terrific influence on every stand-up, one-line monologist. He is also a great screen comic as anyone can tell by looking at his movies like the 'Road' pictures, *Monsieur Beaucaire*, *My Favorite Brunette*, *Son of Paleface* and *Fancy Pants*. The thing which makes him great just can't be stolen or imitated."

WOODY ALLEN
"My Favourite Comedian", May 1979

BOB HOPE

Thanks for the memory

compiled by
Peter Haining

foulsham

LONDON • NEW YORK • TORONTO • SYDNEY

foulsham

Yeovil Road, Slough, Berkshire SL1 4JH

ISBN 0–572–01562–3
Copyright © 1989   Peter Haining

Printed in Great Britain at The Bath Press, Bath.

Contents

Foreword

It is an interesting exercise to notice how many players from this country, especially comedians, are celebrated in American cinema: Charles Chaplin of course, Stan Laurel of the Laurel and Hardy team, and now in Peter Haining's compilation you will find that Bob Hope was originally British. He was born in Eltham; his father came from Barry in South Glamorgan and his mother too was from Wales. Devotedly tracing the family background, Mr. Haining shows that though the boy escaped the rigours of Chaplin's childhood, he grew up in difficult circumstances. In 1907, the family moved to the United States, and for Bob Hope the teenager there were the traditional jobs: paperboy and soda jerk. Mr Haining has found evidence of another role: in a surprising interval Bob Hope made an attempt at a career in boxing. He won no championships luckily for the cinema, and luckily for us there was a discovery. He could dance, he could sing (remember *Thanks for the Memory?*). Above all he could generate and bring off wise cracks. There was vaudeville, and at last there was cinema.

The author makes no mistakes: Bob Hope was never a creative comedian in the way in which Laurel and Hardy were creative. But though he used the jokes supplied by his staff, he could make his own; he could create the atmosphere in which jokes flourished. Everybody remembers the long list of farcical goings on in the one-hero target of *My Favourite Blonde* or *The Paleface*. It was, however, in a partnership that his astonishing gift for the fast irreverent crack won its most durable successes. The 'road' series began in 1940 with *Road to Singapore*, Dorothy Lamour as the beauty, Bob Hope and Bing Crosby (who always got the girl) exchanging insults. There was spontaneous fun, there was a sense of freedom and enjoyment in the playing which is itself creative. There, for me, is the peak of Bob Hope's triumph.

Anyway, thanks for the fun.

Dilys Powell

DILYS POWELL, THE *SUNDAY TIMES.*

ACKNOWLEDGEMENTS

The author is grateful to numerous people for their help in the writing of this book, in particular Bill Lofts, Bob Monkhouse, Gerry Kerr, Linda Matthews and Michael Wilson, as well as the staff of the British Film Institute Reference and Stills Library. He also wishes to acknowledge his thanks to the following publications for permission to quote from their pages: *Sunday Express, Sunday Telegraph, Daily Mail, Daily Telegraph, The Sun, The Western Mail, Daily Express, The Times, The Hitchin Pictorial, The Guardian, Sunday Times, Evening Standard, New York Times, Los Angeles Times, New Statesman, Life, Newsweek, Time, Variety, Photoplay, Film Comment, Rolling Stone, Film Weekly, Picturegoer, Radio Times,* and *TV Guide.* The following also provided photographs for use in the book: British Film Institute, Popperfoto, Solo Picture Agency, Telegraph Newspapers Ltd., Paramount Pictures, Warner Brothers, United Artists and MGM.

1
Hope Springs Eternal

Bob looking for the secret recipe for success? He found it singing the title song of this movie, *Thanks for the Memory* (1938).

Fifty years ago, as the storm clouds of war gathered over the British Isles, Bob Hope the English-born comedian who was to become the "Clown Prince of America", returned to his native land. It was, in fact, the first time the comic, who was on the verge of international stardom after having won acclaim on the theatrical stages and over the air waves of America, had come back to the country he had left with his parents when he was just four years old. (He is the fifth of seven sons, in fact, the others are Jack, George, Ivor, Jim, Sid and Fred, and there was also a daughter, Emily, who died in infancy.)

"The Clown Prince of America" — an unusual photograph of Bob on the set of *Monsieur Beaucaire* (1946) with one of his favourite directors, George Marshall.

Bob's English relatives are mainly concentrated in Hitchin, Hertfordshire, not that far from the London suburb of Eltham where he had been born in 1903, and here he hosted a reunion for the 40-strong clan during the last week of August. "We had a party in a pub in Hitchin," he was to recall years later of this event which helped him fill in details about his origins, "and the MC was my grandfather, James Hope. He was then 96 and he sang a few songs and danced a little jig."

Nor was this to be the only war-time reunion in "old Jolly" — as Hope has often referred to his native land. For fate brought him back for another meeting with that remarkable old man who, along with Bob's mother and father, had been one of the first influences on his life and eventual career in show business.

"I came back again in June 1943 when I was touring military camps during the build up to D-Day," he says. "I was at an RAF Fighter Command Base at Wharton and there he was among all the pilots in the audience. I couldn't believe it. He came down the aisle on his cane. I helped him up on the stage and he wished everyone good luck on their missions.

"That was the last time I saw him," Bob adds. "I was in Birmingham a couple of weeks later when I got the word he had died. It was a month before his 100th birthday."

Longevity is, in fact, not uncommon in the Hope family — an attribute that Bob, who has also been called "America's National Clown", has certainly inherited — still active as he is at the splendid age of 86 as I write this tribute. Of course, as the son of an impoverished stonemason named Harry Hope who quit England to find a better life for his family across the Atlantic, Bob has certainly achieved a great deal in terms of status and wealth since he discovered his talent as a comedian. Not for nothing is he now referred to as "The King of Comics" and "the richest entertainer who has ever lived". He himself perhaps most enjoys being described as "a cross between Father Christmas and the public conscience".

Yet despite his birth in England, there is no denying that Bob Hope is today the quintessential American comic actor — as well as being a fervent American patriot, a friend of Presidents and virtually a national institution. As the English journalist Mark Wilder wrote in May 1983 to mark his 80th birthday, "He is the man who symbolises Yankee brashness and fun — so much so that were America to elect a sovereign this month, he would be King Robert I."

But this said, Bob has maintained on more than one occasion, "I'm really sentimental about England. In fact, I'm crazy about it and I go to a lot of trouble to keep in touch with my roots. Especially the great golf courses!" (He has, in fact, a legendary loyalty to his distant kin and relatives as well as his brothers and old theatrical buddies.)

Bob is one of those rare stars whose names are immediately familiar and whose features are instantly recognisable. A tall man, just under six foot, age may have thinned his rusty auburn hair, but in no way dimmed his brown eyes which have been described as "like milk chocolate buttons about to melt", nor affected the thrust of his nose, often referred to by his late and much-lamented partner, Bing Crosby, as resembling a "ski jump made of flesh". In fact, how he came by his unusual features is rarely referred to in interviews.

The truth is he owes that famous face to an accident in 1921 which came within a heartbeat of taking his life. The then 18-year-old Les Hope (his given names are actually Leslie Towns Hope, changed later for professional reasons as we shall see) was spending a working holiday with his older brother, Jim, at a logging camp in Cuyahoga Valley, Ohio. Sent up a tall pine to tie a rope to the top of the tree which was in the process of being felled, Bob suddenly found the tree overbalancing and falling. Only by split-second thinking and managing to fling himself to the upper side of the tree did he save himself from being crushed under the massive pine when it hit the ground. His handsome young face, though, was slammed against the rough bark of the tree by the whiplash effect.

One of Bob's many awards. He is seen here in 1986 receiving an Honorary Doctorate at the University of Scranton.

"King Robert" of America meets Queen Elizabeth from his native England at the Royal Variety Performance in London in October 1962. The other stars are Sophie Tucker, Ted Shapiro and Edie Adams.

Opposite:
"The richest entertainer who ever lived" — Bob has always been careful with his money and invested wisely.

"I woke up in the hospital and they wouldn't give me a mirror for three weeks," Bob admitted in a rare discussion of this event with Timothy White of *Rolling Stone* in 1980. "I was worried, but I felt lucky to be alive. My family was relieved when they found out there were no brain injuries, but the doctors had to arrange my nose and face. I also had two facial scars afterwards that they've since fixed up."

In hindsight, Bob can agree that while the accident may have changed his features, it also in all probability helped his career. The jutting chin, the prominent nose and the mobile mouth have been used to give irresistible impact to his swift comedy patter. Indeed, English critic David Pitt has precisely summarised the Hope acting *persona* in these words: "His talent is a combination of the visual (the shifty, mobile face) and the oral (the caustic, self-destructive wisecrack) humour."

The American magazine *Time*, in paying tribute to his achievements — and with a neat acknowledgement to his well-known passion for golf — commented a few years back:

"Bob Hope comes on stage with the cocky glide of a golfer who has just knocked off three birdies for a 68 and nailed

'It's a pity Richard Nixon can't take Bob Hope and Dorothy Lamour on his Road to Peking.'

Bob has also been the butt of cartoonists' jokes as well as attacks from media writers and commentators. This example from the Vietnam War era is from the *New Statesman* of 31 December 1971.

Arnold Palmer to the club house door. The crooked grin spreads wide, the clear brown eyes stay cool, and the audience roars its welcome; they can hardly wait for Hope to sock it to them. And so he does.

Five, six gags a minute. Pertinent, impertinent, leering, perishing. And sometimes plopping, but only for an instant. When he misses, the famous scooped snoot shoots defiantly skyward, the prognathous jaw drops in mock anguish, or goes into a stop-action freeze. Sometimes he just repeats the line until the audience gets it. They don't have to laugh of course — but if they don't, it's almost treason."

Time maintained that Bob possesses a special understanding of what is unique in American humour:

"Hope laces his wit with good taste. He may sometimes play the ogling goof, but he is essentially a monologist who portrays no other character than Bob Hope. His comedy is almost always clean, topical, deftly timed and tuned to the sensibilities of his audience . . . What crowds, large or small, recognise is not only a man who has made them laugh but one who, without sentimentality, ostention or ballyhoo has become a national hero."

Indeed, as a result of his quarter of a century of exhausting Christmas visits to the far corners of the earth to cheer soldiers on active duty, he well earned the gold medal awarded by the American Congress and presented by President Kennedy in 1963 as "America's most prized Ambassador of Good Will". Similarly, his 12 years of weekly radio shows, almost 80 films, and more than 300 TV shows, not to mention uncounted theatre shows, many for charity, have earned him virtually every award that show business can bestow, including five "Special" Oscars. (Given not for acting, but for his contributions to the film industry!) In 1976, his achievements were even acknowledged on the other side of the Atlantic when he was made an Honorary Commander of the British Empire. (Interestingly, in Britain, too, his early reputation for telling sexually daring jokes on the radio also gave rise to the Cockney slang expression a "Bob Hope joke", signifying any story with a *double entendre* in it!)

Bob's careful husbanding of his considerable earnings over the years matched to shrewd investment planning has earned him a place in *Fortune* magazine's prestigious listing of the 50 Wealthiest Americans.

Although he has been understandably cagey about discussing just how much he is worth, it is equally true that Bob has donated millions of his dollars to charity over the years. Among the causes he has supported are the American Cancer Society, the Los Angeles Music Centre, and various hospitals, universities and schools, including the Bob Hope High for crippled children in Texas.

He has, though, also invested consistently and soundly in property. One of his first investments was a joint venture with

Bing Crosby into a Texan oil well which brought him in about $3 million. His business firm, Bob Hope Enterprises, now owns 8,000 acres of land in Palm Springs; 7,500 acres in the San Fernando Valley; between 4-5,000 acres near Phoenix, Arizona; and 1,500 acres in Malibu. To this can be added scattered properties in California (at Thousand Oaks near Los Angeles and Burbank among other localities) and in Puerto Rico; plus interests in his home town baseball team, the Cleveland Indians, a horse race track, a dairy business, a metal company and various radio and TV stations.

As a matter of note, when all this property was estimated some years ago by a magazine to give him a net worth of $500 million, Bob responded in typical fashion with a telegram to the editor which read, "If you can find it, we'll go halves."

What he *will* say when pressed about money is fairly pithy. "You can't talk about property you haven't sold in the total of what I'm worth," he maintains. "Audiences don't mind me having money because I always go on and make some joke about tax — that gets them on my side. I need money. I have a staff of 30 and four houses, never mind the government to support!"

It would also be making a mistake to imagine that a man so unfailingly cheerful in public has had a carefree life in private. For over 20 years now he has suffered a recurring problem with his left eye and has undergone four operations. Speaking in 1983, Bob not only talked about these troubles but also revealed another little-known story about his young days.

"The trouble may have started when I was a young man in Cleveland. You see I changed my name to Packy East and became a boxer. I hardly won a fight and the trouble could have started then. [As a result of this revelation, I have investigated the story of 'Bob Hope, boxer' and it appears later in this book.] It might also have been caused by overwork, because I first had this haemorrhage when I was overscheduled and collapsed. I should have had a thorough examination then, but I didn't. So now my vision in the left eye is blurry. I have to rely on cue cards during my performances."

He has also had problems with his back. "I got this pain in my back some time ago and when it persisted I went to a bone specialist who told me I had a worn-out disc. Now I take exercise on the rings to keep my back in order."

Perhaps most serious of all, in 1982 he confessed that he had been drinking too much.

"I was a drinker for a long time, and then I started to get trouble with my bladder. The Doctor told me that if I kept drinking I was eventually going to die from it. So I stopped before it put me in the grave. What really got me off the booze was when the doctor said I wouldn't be able to play golf. There was *no way* I was going to give up golf, so I had to quit drinking!"

"Travelling Hope-fully" 1: The start of the series of cartoons made by Sig Vogt during Bob's world tour with his great friend, Jerry Colonna, to entertain the American Forces in 1944. Nine more sketches from this series will be found later in the book.

"Travelling Hope-fully" 2: Bob and Jerry take ship for Europe from San Francisco.

Danger from other sources has also troubled him. In June 1979, Bob had a narrow escape when he was the target of an amazing kidnap attempt which was discovered just in time by the FBI. When the kidnappers failed to breach Bob's home in Palm Springs, they instead snatched a local millionaire's wife who was released when the ransom was paid.

Bob has also had his fair share of bad publicity — his support for the American presence in Vietnam (which, of course, he frequently visited to give his Christmas shows) was attacked in certain sections of the press which even tried to brand him a war-lover. And some jokes he made about the Falklands War in 1982 drew several hostile letters in the British press.

His resilience and amazing stamina have enabled Bob to bounce back from all these set-backs, helped as he has been by his wife of more than 50 years, Dolores (née Reade) who he married at Christmas 1934. A singer at the Vogue Club in New York when they met, Dolores gave up her career when they married, and has shown herself a strong willed and resourceful woman who has done much to sustain her husband through the self-imposed demands of his work. Talking about Dolores recently, Bob quipped:

"In over fifty years of marriage I've only been home three weeks — that ought to tell you something about my marriage! On my last birthday my wife gave me a gold jewellery box and the inscription read, 'Don't think those three weeks haven't been fun'. No way has our life been dull. I've been around beautiful women, but I always went home for dinner. I didn't work late. There's a lot of love between us. When we wake up in the morning we laugh. We have mutual respect. That's the major ingredient of a good marriage, respect."

The couple have raised four adopted children: Linda, the oldest, who works for her father's TV production company; Anthony, now a lawyer in Washington; Nora, married to a financier; and the youngest, Kelly, who works in a museum in San Francisco.

Bob's wife and family — not to mention his three grand-children — have helped keep him as one of the Peter Pans of show business, and it has been one of the great pleasures of his career that he has continued to appeal to each new generation of young people. Though he is undoubtedly much admired by many of the millions of soldiers whom he entertained during the Second World War and later in Vietnam, teenagers who have only seen him on TV also share this affection.

A British ex-serviceman who remembers seeing several of Bob Hope's concerts during the war, said in a feature written in 1978 to mark the star's 75th birthday:

"He was absolutely tireless in his work for the troops. And whatever some people said about his image of always playing the prototype of the incompetent coward, we

Bob the family man — here with his wife, Dolores, and their four adopted children, Linda, Anthony, Nora and Kelly.

thought he was great. You see, we were all incompetent cowards, and he was just being us as we really were!"

A year after this tribute, in March 1979, Bob was given an even more impressive accolade. The American teenage magazine *Seventeen* announced that ten million young people had put Bob at the top of their popularity poll for "The Most Admired Man in the USA". The veteran comic was then 76 years old and came well ahead of a number of much younger stars including Robert Redford, Burt Reynolds and even John Travolta. A delighted Bob said on hearing this news: "I've always said the greatest asset of any comedian is to have a young mind. I've always tried to keep this. Perhaps people will believe that I'm not just all about nostalgia."

Another asset is his consuming drive to get up and perform. "People wonder why I work so hard," he told an interviewer a few years ago. "It's not work. I love what I do. The greatest thing in the world is laughs. Laughs are excitement."

Just how this remarkable man in his eighties has kept his enduring popularity along the path he has walked from a humble birth on the outskirts of London to a sumptuous, futuristic building in Palm Springs where he now happily lives, is what will be found in the pages which follow . . .

2

From Craigton Road to Palm Springs

"My dad was a sort of an amateur comedian, and he would go round and play a few pubs in England and have a few drinks with the boys. My mother was a concert singer in Wales before she got married."

Bob Hope, 1980

Leslie Towns Hope, the child destined to become Bob Hope, was born on 29 May 1903, just two years after the death of Queen Victoria. The son of William Henry Hope, a master stonemason, and Iris Hope (formerly Towns), he came into the world at 44 Craigton Road in Eltham, then a suburb some ten miles from the centre of London but now virtually swallowed up by the metropolis.

The house in Craigton Road, a tiny three-bedroom terrace property with an outside lavatory and covered-up bath in the kitchen, was a typical labourer's home little different from thousands of others which had been built on the outskirts of London during the latter part of the Victorian era. Though the life of the Hope family was by no stretch of the imagination as tough and unrelentingly harsh as that of another equally famous London family, the Chaplins, who a little earlier had also given the world another great entertainer, it was to force them to pack up and head across the Atlantic four years after Bob's birth to seek a better life.

That the young Hope was to become an entertainer seems virtually predestined. For beyond Eltham, the roots of his parents lay in Wales, the great land of song. Interestingly, too, both the home in which Bob's mother was born in Barry and his own birthplace in Eltham survive to this day and are little changed from those days of his infancy. And, starting

Bob Hope's parents, Harry and Iris, taken at the time of their wedding in Wales in 1891.

18

CERTIFIED COPY OF AN ENTRY OF BIRTH

GIVEN AT THE GENERAL REGISTER OFFICE, LONDON.

Application Number R125259

	REGISTRATION DISTRICT Lewisham								
1903. BIRTH in the Sub-district of Eltham					in the County of London				
Columns:—	1	2	3	4	5	6	7	8	9	10*
No.	When and where born	Name, if any	Sex	Name, and surname of father	Name, surname, and maiden surname of mother	Occupation of father	Signature, description and residence of informant	When registered	Signature of registrar	Name entered after registration
53	Twenty ninth May 1903 44 Craigton Road Eltham	Leslie Towns	Boy	William Henry Hope	Iris Hope formerly Towns	Stone-mason (master)	Iris Hope mother 44 Craigton Road Eltham	Tenth July 1903	J.R.S. Murphy Registrar	

CERTIFIED to be a true copy of an entry in the certified copy of a Register of Births in the District above mentioned.

Given at the GENERAL REGISTER OFFICE, LONDON, under the Seal of the said Office the, 30th day of September 1988.

*See note overleaf.

BCA 232183

This certificate is issued in pursuance of the Births and Deaths Registration Act 1953.

Section 34 provides that any certified copy of an entry purporting to be sealed or stamped with the seal of the General Register Office shall be received as evidence of the birth or death to which it relates without any further or other proof of the entry, and no certified copy purporting to have been given in the said Office shall be of any force or effect unless it is sealed or stamped as aforesaid.

CAUTION:—It is an offence to falsify a certificate or to make or knowingly use a false certificate or a copy of a false certificate intending it to be accepted as genuine to the prejudice of any person, or to possess a certificate knowing it to be false without lawful authority.

Birth certificate of Leslie Towns Hope, born in Eltham in 1903.

with them, we can trace the life of Bob Hope from his humble South London origins to the multi-millionaire lifestyle he now enjoys in Palm Springs, the home of some of the wealthiest men and women in the world.

The Hopes are actually a very old English family, the first recorded member being a Roger de la Hope who was alive in 1273. It appears they got their name originally from some people who lived in a sloping hollow between two hills that was called a "Hope".

Genealogist W.O.G. Lofts, who has tracked down the family trees of many famous entertainers over the years, has discovered that Bob Hope's branch of the family seems to have originated from the West Country of England. There is, he says, a row of "Hope" cottages which were probably built by one of his ancestors in Bath about 150 years ago — which ties in neatly with the profession of stonemason which Bob's father and his grandfather had followed. Lofts goes on:

"By all accounts the family seem to have been blessed with long lives. Dozens of Hopes have lived to be over 90 as well as two who were 101 and 100 when they died. Bob's grandfather only missed out by one month — being 99 years and 11 months when he passed away. What a pity to be so close to receiving a telegram of congratulations from King George VI!"

Bob himself has commented, "Family has always meant a lot to me. The Hopes, whether of Eltham, England, or Cleveland, Ohio, had a strong clannish instinct. They stuck together: facing tough times always binds people closer — and the Hopes had many a battle on their hands."

Tracing the part of the Hope family tree which most interests us takes us back to the late 1800s and the Welsh seaport of Barry in South Glamorgan. Here, at 12 Greenwood Street, a tiny, three-bedroom house facing towards the port, lived Iris Towns, orphaned as an infant and being raised by a retired sea captain named Lloyd whose life had benefited immeasurably since 1880 when Barry had become an important coal-exporting port. Iris was a small, dark-haired, rather delicate girl with a shy manner and a typically lyrical Welsh voice who sang at local halls.

Talking years later about the woman who was to be his mother, Bob said, "My mother was a concert singer and I inherited my voice from her. She used to sit me on her lap when I was small and teach me Welsh hymns. I had a lovely Michael Jackson voice until I was 14. Then it broke and I had to get out of the girls' choir," he added, unable to resist a quick joke.

In 1890, a young man named Harry Hope, who was then working as a stonemason in the Barry Docks, first saw Iris Towns and fell in love. In the months which followed he came courting to 12 Greenwood Street, and winning the girl's heart, asked Mr. Lloyd's permission to marry. On 25 April 1891, the couple were married in Cardiff.

Today, the house in Greenwood Street bears a small plaque, "William Henry Hope, father of the famous comedian, Bob Hope, lived here". In October 1984, the house was actually visited by Bob during a concert tour which brought him to Cardiff. The occupants, pensioners Raymond and Martha-Ann Davies, said afterwards, "We told him everything about the house and joked about how his father had courted his mother here." Bob himself commented, "It was a very emotional moment for me. I'm part Welsh, so it was a real homecoming."

Despite the work that was available for the Hopes in Barry at the turn of the century, William Hope with his growing family decided soon afterwards to move South where his father — Bob's much-loved "Grandpop James" — was a general contractor and forever in need of more men. The family purchased the stone-built terrace house at 44 Craigton Road (reputedly built by grandfather Hope), Henry paying £198 and securing a mortgage of £110. Here, a short walk from Eltham High Street, Leslie Towns Hope was born in May 1903 — named after a relative who had served with General Gordon in the Sudan in 1884.

By a curious twist of fate, two landmarks stand within walking distance of the house, both of which were to figure large in the life of the newly-born infant: the Eltham Little Theatre and the Royal Blackheath Golf Course. Bob was later to make significant appearances at both.

The hopes remained at number 44 for just two more years before moving again to Bristol, and Bob admits candidly that he remembers very little about his days in Eltham. It was in that house, however, that he first came under the influence of his grandfather who was to encourage his inherent acting talent.

"My brother Ivor told me that Grandpop used to put me on a table and make me dance or sing or play a tune on a comb covered with tissue paper. He swears that for some reason Grandpop called me 'Tin Ribs'."

A rare and faded photograph of Bob, aged four, at the time his parents were emigrating to America.

Bob actually discovered more about his past when he revisited the house for the first time in 1980. He had actually tried to find the place some five years before when he had been in the country for a Royal Variety performance — but his search had ended in disaster. He explains:

"I'd gone to play on the Royal Blackheath Golf Course which is just along the street from where I was born. I thought I was born at number 25, Craigton Road. So I went to this house and knocked on the door. I wish I had it on film. This couple came out. I said, 'How are you?' 'OK. How are you?' they said. 'I'm Bob Hope,' I said. 'Yes'. 'I was born here' 'Really?' They gave me all the welcome of someone selling bicycle clips or something. It turned out I was at the wrong house!"

Then, in September 1980, while in England to play in the Bob Hope British Golf Classic, Bob successfully found his birthplace. He was enthusiastically welcomed by the owners,

A legend returns to his roots — Bob outside his birthplace, 44 Craigton Road, Eltham, in September 1980, with the occupants, John and Flo Ching, and their neighbour, Elsie Woodbine.

John and Florence Ching — Mrs. Ching's mother having actually bought the property for £250 from Bob's father and then later sold it to the couple for £650. The Chings in fact still have the title deeds to the house bearing the signature of William Henry Hope.

Bob quickly explained to the couple his previous error. "The houses were so close together it's difficult to tell which is mine. My father was very confused about that. He was always going into the wrong house. Mind you, he had a lot of fun!"

The comedian was given a conducted tour of the premises which, his hosts said, were little changed from the days when the Hopes lived there. In the back garden Bob saw a huge pear tree and vaguely recalled having tried to climb it and being soundly spanked by his mother. An older brother had told him that their father, who was a bit of sports lover, had kept gamecocks in the garden and fought them against other birds — a sport long since outlawed.

"I can't really remember how the house looked then," he told the Chings. "We left here when I was three. But I'm always pleased to have the chance to come back to England."

According to a story Bob told in 1953, he gave his first "performance" while he was in Eltham. In an interview with the British Sunday newspaper *Reynolds News* he said,

"I first made my theatrical appearance in 1906. I was sent to a local Eltham hospital with scarlet fever and put in an isolation ward. On visitors' day I sneaked out from solitary and ran all over the hospital pulling funny faces. Everyone laughed. But it was soon cut short when the doctors announced that everyone I'd had contact with would have to stay in quarantine for several weeks. I doubt whether I should be forgotten in Eltham even if I had not become a comedian!"

In September 1982 Bob was back in Eltham again, this time accompanied by his wife Dolores, to visit the town's 280-seat theatre which had been saved from being demolished through a donation of £58,500 from the Bob Hope British Golf Classic — and as a result was to be renamed The Bob Hope Theatre. He unveiled a plaque and bust of himself — and delighted the invited audience with a string of jokes about the English weather and the fact that as he had been born in the country and was now 79 he was surely entitled to a bus pass! And when he was briefly interrupted by a baby's cry from the back stalls of the theatre he responded with a nice line: "Was that my echo?"

When he was again questioned about his early days in England, Bob said,

"There's only one really clear memory, and that's about Bristol where we moved before going to America. I was protecting my dog from some children who were throwing stones and I got hit on the head. You can still see the mark."

"Travelling Hope-fully" 3: Bob and Jerry meet the famous 'Little Dutch Boy'.

Bob unveiling a bust of himself in the Eltham Little Theatre, which was re-named The Bob Hope Theatre in September 1982.

Bob's brother Ivor has also told another dramatic story of the youngster at this period of his life. Apparently when the family were having a short holiday at Herne Bay in Kent, Bob splashed into the sea and but for Ivor's quick action would have drowned. His high spirits were obviously quite capable of getting him into trouble even at that early age!

It was, though, in 1907 that William Hope decided to leave England and go to Cleveland to pursue his trade as a stone-mason. The rest of the family finally departed for New York the next year, arriving in March 1908. During the crossing, Bob is said to have so resented the idea of being vaccinated, that he ran away from the doctor and started a Keystone Cops-like chase around the decks until he was finally grabbed!

Of the Hope residence in Bristol, Bob has said, "It was pretty small like the one in Eltham. But Dad had a high brick wall put around it for privacy — something I've also had to do at my own place in Palm Springs!"

The palatial and futuristic house which Bob has built in Palm Springs — a world away from the terraces of Eltham!

The Palm Springs house is, indeed, a palace fit for a King of comedy, and viewing it even from a distance underlines just how far the stonemason's son from Eltham has come. A futuristic looking building, it sits like a giant mushroom on a granite outcrop of a mountain high above this wealthy Californian desert enclave. Entering it up a cascade of black marble stairs under a wide-vaulting arch, a visitor's first impression is of walking into some gigantic award-winning film set.

The domed, circular roof covers 25,000 square feet with a 60 foot wide skylight in the middle. There is a massive living room dominated by a fireplace ten feet across, flanked by boulders and with a hood soaring 30 feet up to the curved roof. The bedroom areas of the house are the size of small flats, there is a kitchen big enough to serve a restaurant, and a dining room with a table to seat 20 people. Inside, too, is a large indoor garden complete with a waterfall, and a luxurious billiard room. In the carefully manicured grounds outside can be found a swimming pool and Bob's pride and joy, a perfectly laid out one-hole golf course.

The house, conceived by an old friend, interior decorator Arthur Elrod, took nine years to complete. At one stage it was almost abandoned after a fire virtually destroyed the half-built property and then Elrod himself was killed in a traffic accident. For a time a thoroughly dispirited Bob felt like selling up, but is now very glad he had the job completed.

The views from the property of the surrounding mountains are breathtakingly spectacular, and because the complex itself can be seen for miles around, Bob jokes that "Pilots flying overhead call it TWA West!"

Bob also owns two other houses in Palm Springs, a country house in Columbus, Ohio, and a 15-room ranch-house style property at Toluca Lake near Hollywood which he has owned for almost half a century and from which Bob Hope Enterprises have long been run.

It is from the grandeur of the spaceship-like home in Palm Springs that Bob can look back on a lifetime of achievement since he left England and found America to be the land of

Bob enjoying a light-hearted moment with two of his children, Linda and Anthony, in the grounds of one of his other homes in Hollywood.

opportunity that everyone talked of. He likes to joke about the reason why he emigrated.

"I wasn't getting anywhere," he has quipped, "and I realised I'd never be King." And: "What would have happened if I'd have stayed in England? I have so much talent I still would have made it." Doubtless true. But nothing, in fact, detracts from Bob's obvious affection for Britain and its people. "I love London," he will tell any listener. "You know, I've drunk so much tea there I slosh when I walk!"

One thing Bob has retained from his childhood *is* his love of a walk. And he still takes a stroll every night from his home towards Palm Springs, usually dressed in one of his favourite golf shirts, a pair of check trousers and some comfortable white loafers. On a recent stroll, he was accompanied by journalist, E. Graydon Carter, who recorded afterwards:

"The constant in Hope's day is his nightly walk. It is the vaudevillian's instinct that the moment you are off the stage the audience begins to forget you, and so Hope works even here. He window shops and scratches autographs on cocktail napkins, all without breaking his stride. Amid his endless patter of 'Howyadooins', the giggling of three teen-age girls catches Hope's attention. Chirping and darting looks at one another, the youngsters ask him the way to a local nightspot. Hope savours the moment, then points the direction. As he watches them wiggle off into the night, he nudges his companion and whispers out of the side of his mouth, 'What do you think? You want to go dancing?'"

A remark so international it might be heard just as easily on a street in Eltham any night. The links between the Bob Hope of today and his origins are, despite his fame and wealth, still as close as that. He remains the man on "The Road to Everywhere".

"Travelling Hope-fully" 4: Drama with an aeroplane engine during the flight to Australia.

3
The Fall and Fall of Packy East

Bob Hope, boxer — squaring up to former world champion Jack Dempsey, for a TV special in 1951.

One of the most curious and little-know episodes in Bob Hope's life is the brief period in 1920 when he attempted to carve out a career for himself as a boxer.

There is no mention of this unlikely diversion in any of his biographies and indeed whenever Bob has been questioned by journalists about his pugilistic achievements he has been typically flippant — though it is true to say that he has had a lifelong interest in boxing and has attended numerous big fights in America over the years, as well as watching the sport regularly on television.

The facts about Bob Hope, boxer, require some digging out, but are basically as follows. It was Bob's father, the sturdy, mustacheod stonemason who had worked with his powerful hands all his life and was a sportsman by instinct who

introduced all his sons to boxing. Bob, apparently, got his first taste of the sport even before he left England.

Talking in 1954, Bob said, "My brother Ivor remembers father teaching us to box down in the cellar of our house in Bristol. He used to hold out his chin at us and say, 'Hit it!'"

When the Hope family settled in Cleveland in 1908, Bob says that times were hard for them at home and no easy matter for him at school. "There was not as much work around for my father as he had thought, and at times he grew so discouraged he took to the bottle," Bob has recalled. "My dear mother worked so hard supporting us, dressing us and keeping us fed. We were average financially, I guess, but we had to fight it out and everybody had to work."

At school, Bob found his English accent the butt of jokes from other pupils, and even when he declared in tones that he hoped sounded American that his name was "Les Hope", he found this quickly turned into a nick-name that stuck for some years: "Hopeless".

But Bob was not afraid to use his fists, and joining up with a local gang got involved in any number of typical boyish pranks like scrumping apples and taunting authority.

As soon as he reached his teens, Bob started to play his part in bringing money into the house. He first tried his hand as a newspaper seller and shortly had a traumatic encounter with a customer that was to influence his philosophy towards work and money for the rest of his life.

One day as he stood on a street corner an old gentleman, who was not one of his regular customers, stopped to buy a paper. The man did not have the right money and the boy had no change.

"Pay me tomorrow," said Bob, "I'll trust you, sir." But, much to the young seller's surprise, the man refused and insisted that Bob *get* some change. This meant running all the way up the street and losing more customers while he got the money. But on his return, the young newspaper seller was given a piece of very valuable advice.

"One thing you must always remember," the man said as the out-of-breath young Hope handed him his change, "Never give credit when you can get cash."

The man, it transpired, was none other than the multi-millionaire John D. Rockefeller — and this anecdote has been frequently cited as the inspiration for the shrewd money sense which has since made Bob Hope a multimillionaire himself!

But times did not immediately improve for Bob and after his paper job he was also a baker's delivery boy, a soda jerk, shoe salesman and even, briefly, a dance instructor when he discovered a talent for the soft-shoe shuffle. Then, from the age of 19, he was a clerk with the Chandler Motor Car Company. Here Bob made his first "record" — using the office manager's dictating machine to listen to himself singing "Sweet Rosie O'Grady". But when he forgot to erase his voice one night, his association with Chandler came to an abrupt end the next morning!

"Travelling Hope-fully" 5: An uncomfortable landing for Jerry Colonna in New Guinea.

It was after this string of less than successful periods of employment that Bob decided to try his luck as a boxer. Apart from the lessons from his father, and the scraps in the schoolyard, he had also received some coaching in a neighbourhood gym. So, plucking up courage, the young Hope entered himself for his first contest under the unlikely sounding name of Packy East. The name had apparently been derived from a well-known fighter named Packy McFarland.

The indications are clear that his career in the ring was short-lived as his own few comments on this aspect of his life have shown. But, as the records reveal, not so completely disastrous as he would have us believe.

In an interview with *Reynolds News* in 1953 he said cagily, "I had a couple of fights and hit the other fellow so hard with my chin that I woke up in the dressing room. After that it got spread around — rather horribly I thought — that 'Packy East' was the nose on the arena floor. So I gave up fighting. You see, I wasn't even making hospital expenses. They should have told me they wanted me to fight men!"

A *Time* magazine writer got nothing more substantial when he raised the subject in 1979. "Boxing was where I learned to waltz," the comedian said. "I was the only guy they carried into the ring as well as out of it."

And in 1983, to another British paper, *The News of the World*, he was only prepared to joke, "When I was a boxer they should have called me Rembrandt East, not Packy East. After all, I spent most of my time on the canvas!"

In fact, Packy East actually *won* his first bout against another boy called Jim Holmes, going three rounds before the fight was stopped in his favour.

His next match proved a very different proposition, however. He was put in the ring with a lad named "Happy" Walsh whose name quite belied his disposition. He dumped Bob on the floor three times before knocking him out in the second round. It was this beating that convinced young Bob that any aspirations he might have to be a contender were ill-founded. ("Happy" Walsh, in fact, went on to become a Cleveland champion.)

However, hauling himself back onto his feet, Bob decided there must be a less painful way of getting laughs. Perhaps show business was the answer, he wondered? From his father he had learned to tap dance and do impersonations, and, of course, his mother had taught him singing and the importance of timing. There had always been the encouragement of Grandpop Hope, too, who had also followed the family to America — though he later returned to Hitchin.

"He was such a good old guy," Bob recalled, "very witty, full of cracks and always ready to put on a little show. He was a great encouragement in bringing the comic out in me."

So, at the tender age of 21, Bob left home to seek his fortune, having placed an advertisement in the show business newspaper *Variety*, which read: "LES HOPE available. Songs, patter and eccentric dances."

Bob with two of his partners on the road to fame (above) with an attractive dancer, Hilda, who he wanted to take on tour until her mother objected! and (right) with his soft-shoe pal, Lloyd "Lefty" Durbin.

As the now famous legend of Bob Hope recounts, the response to this advertisement was virtually nil, and because he felt that Les Hope still had more than a little association with that school nick-name of "Hopeless", he decided to change it for what he believed was the "chummier" and better-sounding Bob Hope.

Success, though, had to be hard won in the years which followed as he first appeared as half of a two-man dance team, Hope and Durbin, in small concert halls across America; and then on his own in vaudeville where he finally gave vent to his rare gift for wise-cracking comedy. Public recognition at last came for Bob in 1929 when he landed a role in the Broadway musical *Roberta*, and this was followed by parts in several more successful stage shows in the early thirties.

In 1934, he also began doing vaudeville skits on the radio in "The Capitol Family Hour" and by 1937 he had his own weekly programme, "The Woodbury Soap Show". A year later he was a major radio personality with his show for Pepsodent toothpaste and had also broken into films. In the movie *The Big Broadcast of 1938* he sang what thereafter became his theme tune, "Thanks for the Memory". And as the Second World War broke out in Europe, international fame came his way through a starring role in the comedy horror film *The Cat and the Canary*, and the first of the enduringly popular series of Road movies with Bing Crosby and Dorothy Lamour.

In America, his verbal sparring with Crosby over the radio had become essential listening for millions — and transferring this unique banter to the screen opened it up to a worldwide audience. It was also during the war, from May 1941, that Bob began the first of thousands of special shows for the armed forces. Initially these were relayed by radio and later on TV, and continued for over 30 years spanning three wars.

Though it is quite evident that Bob was never destined to be a boxer, his long life and predominantly good health can in

Bob first achieved widespread fame in America on the radio with his own show.

31

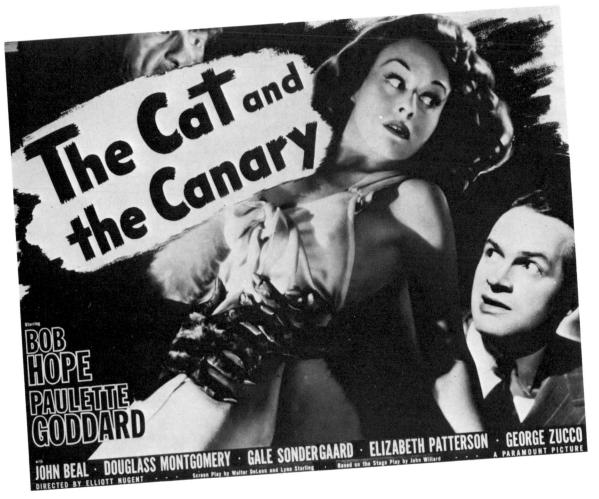

The Cat and the Canary

Starring
BOB HOPE
PAULETTE GODDARD

with JOHN BEAL · DOUGLASS MONTGOMERY · GALE SONDERGAARD · ELIZABETH PATTERSON · GEORGE ZUCCO
DIRECTED BY ELLIOTT NUGENT · · · Screen Play by Walter DeLeon and Lynn Starling · Based on the Stage Play by John Willard · · · · A PARAMOUNT PICTURE

A mixture of straight acting and comedy in the movie that gained Bob recognition on both sides of the Atlantic, the haunted house spoof, *The Cat and the Canary*.

the main be attributed to the care he has taken of himself and the fact he has continued to work out regularly in his own gym, especially on the demanding exercise rings. There are several other stories told about Bob which illustrate both the amusing and serious side of his interest in boxing.

Jerry Colona, his long time co-star on radio and in the touring shows for American servicemen, recalls going to a boxing match with him in Pearl Harbor in 1944.

"We were invited to attend this boxing show at the Nimitz Bowl and we hadn't been seated for more than a minute when word got around that Bob Hope and I were at the ringside. We rose, took a few bows, and climbed into the ring. We wound up flat on our backs. They had forgotten to stop the fight. Hope said this was the first time he had ever been hit before he said anything! I have to admit Bob looked at home in the ring. In a way he is a middleweight champion. He has a lot of weight around the middle!"

Bob was also for many years a friend of the great American heavyweight boxing champion Joe Louis, and the two men often played golf together. Another world champion, Jack

Dempsey, became a friend, too, and in October 1951 Bob climbed into a ring again for the first time for an exhibition "match" with Dempsey as the highlight of one of his TV specials. It was also the first time Dempsey had put on boxing gloves since his retirement — but the sparring performance both men gave delighted the estimated nationwide audience of 50 million viewers!

In February 1968, Bob was again invited into the ring for the opening of the new Madison Square Garden arena in New York. This time he squared up to Rocky Marciano, while his radio and film sparring partner, Bing Crosby, acted as the referee! Bob's "second" was the beautiful actress Barbara Eden. It was one of those days, the newspapers reported afterwards, when Bing yet again "put one over" on Bob!

In 1981, Bob was seen on television with arguably the greatest of all American boxing champions, the multi-world title holder Sugar Ray Leonard. Sugar Ray tells a very interesting tale about Bob's prowess in the ring.

"Mr. Hope asked me to be on his 78th Birthday Special at West Point. He was a boxer when he was a kid so he wanted to do a number in the show sparring with me in the ring. At the time I was the welterweight champion of the world.

Well, I showed up and he was rehearsing with Mickey Rooney. At about 6 p.m. I got in the ring and began to

Bob in the ring again: facing Rocky Marciano in February 1968 at the opening of Madison Square Garden in New York with Bing Crosby as referee! The attractive "second" is Barbara Eden.

World Champion Sugar Ray Leonard taking it on the jaw while rehearsing for the TV Special in which he appeared with Bob in 1981.

work with Bob. He kept saying, 'We can do this better. Let's try it again.' And together we must have done about a dozen rounds.

After about two hours I said to the producer, Jim Lipton, 'I'm getting a little tired. Can't I go back to the hotel for a while?' Lipton said, 'Sure'. I said, 'How old did you say that guy is?' He said, 'He's going to be 78.' I said, 'How long has he been rehearsing today?' He said, 'About twelve hours.'

Just as Lipton was about to go, I asked, 'How much longer is he going to rehearse now?' The producer said, 'About another two hours — he's working on his monologue'. I said, 'Oh brother! That old man wore me out.'"

Many other stars who have worked with Bob Hope on his shows can testify to his enormous energy and to his enthusiasm for keeping fit. As he himself once put it, "I'd rather wear out than rust!"

Looking back across 60 years, it is perhaps easy to see that "Packy East" was never going to be a world beater, but the Bob Hope who rose from the canvas of defeat in Cleveland has certainly became one of the champions of show business!

4
A Song Brought Him Fame

In 1939, the first time Bob Hope had returned to England since his family had emigrated, he received his first major publicity feature on the other side of the Atlantic in the leading magazine *Film Weekly*. Here is that milestone article by Lionel Clynton, from the issue of 21 January 1939.

A year or so ago, there blew into Hollywood a young man with an attractive brunette wife, a big radio reputation and an engaging personality.

His name was Bob Hope and his radio reputation was responsible for his being signed up for the screen.

Paramount had induced him to join the other air favourites in *Big Broadcast of 1938*.

He didn't have an overwhelming amount to do in the picture. But he had a song. It was "Thanks for the Memory," which he sang with Shirley Ross.

Now "Thanks for the Memory" is his broadcasting signature tune. He has made a picture with the name of the song as its title—*Thanks for the Memory*. He finds it impossible to get away from the number.

Not that he minds. That one tune has shot him to screen stardom.

Already, he has appeared in *Swing, Teacher, Swing, Give Me a Sailor* (released next week) and *Never Say Die* in addition to *Thanks for the Memory*.

Publicity still for Bob's first starring role in a movie, *The Big Broadcast of 1938*, which featured the great comedian, W.C. Fields.

FIRST A DANCER

He is primarily a wisecracking comedian of the Jack Benny type, though he first established himself in the theatrical world as a dancer.

Ruby Keeler was partly responsible for giving him his first big Broadway chance.

He had teamed up with another dancer, George Byrne, and they had been doing vaudeville work. Then came an audition for an important Broadway musical.

The selection committee was composed of several of New York's topline and most sternly critical stars. Ruby Keeler was one of them.

Several other dancers were being tested. Hope and Byrne waited impatiently and nervously.

Time went on. A clock struck midnight and they began to wonder whether it was worth waiting any longer.

Then, at one o'clock, their names were called. They did their stuff.

A little over twelve hours later, they were signed up for the show.

FAR FROM HANDSOME

On looks alone, it's doubtful whether Bob Hope would have made much progress, especially on the screen. He has a humorous sort of face which no stretch of imagination could consider handsome.

But his personality is unusual. He is breezy and amusing but there is something besides this. It is an air of genuine friendliness.

It's natural to him. He is a man whose belief is that worry should be eliminated from life. It never does any good, however bad the spot you're in.

He should know. Life has not been entirely without troubles for him.

One of his first jobs was that of dancing instructor but he threw this up and took a clerical post in a motor car company.

It was here that his ability as an entertainer was first revealed. He acted as master of ceremonies at the company's conventions, meetings and various other shows. This gave him the idea of going on the stage.

His first stage tour flopped after a couple of weeks. He had linked up with George Byrne and the two had succeeded in getting a booking as supporting act to Fatty Arbuckle, who was making a personal appearance tour.

When the tour was cancelled after two weeks, they wondered what to do next. Luck, however, came their way. Arbuckle introduced them to a musical comedy manager and this led to another stage job.

This time, they did a black-face act, and Bob sang as well as danced. The pay wasn't much, but the tour lasted quite a time.

When it ended, the team of Hope and Byrne went into

Opposite:
A dangerous moment for Bob in the appropriately named film, *Never Say Die* (1939), about to fight a duel with Alan Mowbrey.

"Travelling Hope-fully" 6: A spot of rather unusual fishing for Jerry and Bob off the Pacific Island of Tulagi.

vaudeville, and eventually got the Broadway job I have already mentioned.

EMPTY STOMACH

At the end of this show, they returned to vaudeville, and pure chance led to the changing of Bob's career.

The manager of a theatre asked him one night if he would announce the following week's presentation.

Hope did so in such an entertaining manner that the announcement resolved itself into quite an act. He got a big hand from the audience.

His alert mind got to work. He saw a future for himself as a compère.

He was an instinctive master of ceremonies. He always found it easy to fit amusing stories to any situation.

He decided to try his luck in this field. The Hope-Byrne act was broken up. He set off on his own.

The decision cost him quite a lot of money and heartache. He got a few jobs here and there in night clubs, at private parties and small theatres.

But he didn't earn enough to keep body and soul together. He had to keep on borrowing money to see him through.

He refused to change his plans, however. He was convinced that one day he would make a success of compère work.

So he went on cracking jokes in "small time," and an empty stomach didn't impair his sense of humour in the least.

He struck his worst patch in Chicago. He had hoped that he would get some opportunities there; but he couldn't get an audition.

One day, he sat down on a park bench and totalled up his debts. They amounted to about £800. The chances of repaying the money looked very slender indeed.

CHANGE OF LUCK

His shoes needed repairing. He hadn't had a square meal for weeks.

Then, abruptly, luck changed. He met an old friend. The friend invited him to have some dinner.

Hope tucked into an enormous steak with gusto. His friend watched him, then asked: "Having a tough time?"

He nodded. "Pretty tough. There doesn't seem to be anything doing."

But there was something doing. The friend introduced him to an agent.

Within a few days, Bob Hope was working again — as a M.C. at a small theatre. The theatre was one of a chain, and Hope was booked for some of the larger theatres.

There was no stopping him after that. He remained in Chicago for six months, then toured, and landed up in

Looking ahead to greater things? —
Bob with co-star Martha Raye in
Give Me A Sailor, a picture he made
in 1938.

New York with all his debts paid off and a balance of
£1,000 in the bank.

BORN IN LONDON

He was given a three-year contract with the R-K-O-Radio
circuit, which was followed by his appearance in the
"Ziegfeld Follies" and other Broadway shows. Then he went
on the radio and established an even bigger reputation for
himself.

He fell in love and married, and then came Hollywood.

He is typical of the American school of wisecracking,
breezy comedians. But he is English by birth. He was born
in London.

His parents, however, migrated to America when he was
still a toddler, taking him with them. He has, therefore,
been brought up in America and has lived there practically
all his life.

Now, having established himself there, his fame is at last
reaching his native country.

5
A
Star
Returns

Bob surrounded by his relatives on his return to Eltham in 1943.

When Bob made a second return visit to Britain in 1943, his arrival made headlines in all the national newspapers for he was now an acknowledged world star. During his stay, he took time for a reunion with his relatives in Hitchin, thereby creating a tradition he has always observed when crossing the Atlantic. A rare newspaper cutting from the *Hitchin Pictorial* of 29 June describes the star's "surprise visit", and reveals some interesting facts about his relatives in the town.

Was the visit of Bob Hope, the Eltham-born American film and radio star, to Hitchin on Saturday afternoon, less than 24 hours after landing from a Clipper, just the preliminary to the more important call on August 21 when Mr. James Hope, his grandfather, celebrates his 100th birthday?

If so, then this happy reunion with the cheary old man achieved all that it set out to do.

A romantic halo seemed to enshrine the 99-years-old and his happy grandson as they embraced affectionately at the gateway entrance to the old man's home — 146, Bearton-road.

The number of local people to greet Bob Hope was smaller than it would have been had there been some pre-Press publicity.

He had a typically British welcome apart from the family re-union at the home of Mrs. Symons, and the Union Jacks were much in evidence.

When Mr. Hope learned that his famous grandson was coming he got busy, and made strenuous attempts to borrow an American flag, but met with no success.

It was the men and not the flags that mattered.

A Public Relations Officer of the U.S. Army, Capt. W. W. McCoy, met Bob Hope on the latter's arrival, and helped to shepherd the Press photographers, who included

OBITUARY

Mr. James Hope

Mr. James Hope, 99-year-old grandfather of the famous Bob Hope, died on Saturday evening, almost exactly a month before he would have reached his hundredth birthday.

Hitchin's grand old man passed peacefully away, in the presence of his two daughters, Mrs Lucy Symons, with whom he had been living for the past 30 years, and Mrs. F. Paull, who had lately arrived from Southampton.

Half-an-hour previously, his sons, Messrs. Jack and Percy Hope, and his granddaughter, Mrs. Doris Snoad, who with other members of the family, had been tending him constantly, had been present.

Almost the last word that Mr. Hope said was "Bob", to his famous grandson, who arrived on Thursday and left the following day.

It was only on July 1, that Mr. James Hope, with Bob, appeared on the stage at the Regal Cinema, Watford — a little surprise initiated by the "West Herts Post" and the "Pictorial". Mr. Hope received a tumultuous reception. It was Bob's first appearance on a tour of the cinemas in England.

Bob had previously visited his grandfather less than 24 hours after landing in this country from a clipper. This was on June 27, when Mr. James Hope was the chief participant in an informal concert-tea outside the house.

Born at Bath, Mr. James Hope lived a full and happy life. Among the things he has seen is the Statue of Liberty in two places—in France, and in New York, where it was taken later. He leaves two daughters and five sons, 30 grandchildren and several great grandchildren.

Bob's first visit to his grandfather from America, where he went at the age of four, was as a £1,000 a week screen and radio star in August, 1939.

The funeral will take place at Hitchin Parish Church at 10.30 a.m. to-morrow, Wednesday.

Mr. S. Schulman, an American U.S. Army correspondent.

Mr. James Hope proudly displayed his medal awarded to him in recognition of his 50 years' membership of the Amalgamated Union of British Trade Workers, and Bath, where he was born, and Hitchin, where he has spent the greater part of his life, should be proud of him.

In his working life Mr. Hope was a builder, and he helped to erect Letchworth Garden City's first houses.

Accompanying Bob Hope on this memorable occasion were Tony Romano, the famous guitarist member of Skinny Ennis's band who accompanies many of Bob Hope's songs, Jack Pepper, a versatile comedian, who is taking Jerry Colonna's place on this tour to American troop stations, and Mr. Bill Dover, head of the United Service organisation which arranges shows for United States troops.

One of the most amusing and thrilling scenes was Tony and Jack sitting on a food bin outside the house while Bob was having tea inside. To the guitar accompaniment they sang popular numbers, and what artists they proved to be!

Never has such a scene been witnessed in a Hitchin street before, and probably its like will never be seen again.

Bob stayed about an hour, and members of the family present were Mrs. Lucy Symons, who is immortalised in one of Bob's films, and Mrs. F. Paull, of Southampton, daughter of Mr. James Hope; Mr. and Mrs. C. H. Snoad, and their son Keith, aged 4; Mrs. John Gower, and her children, John, Ivor and Lucy Ann; and Mrs. Frank Symons, and her two children, Audrey and Jean.

The visit was such a surprise that there was no time to arrange for Mr. James Hope's two sons, Jack, of Letchworth, and Percy, of Holwell, to be present, but no doubt all will meet on the great day of celebration next month.

Postscript

Sadly, James Hope, Bob's grandfather, was to die on 24 July while his famous grandson was still in the country — and just one month before he would have reached the fabled age of 100. An account of the old man's death, also in the *Hitchin Pictorial* of 27 July, records: "Almost the last word that Mr. Hope said was 'Bob', to his famous grandson, who arrived on Thursday and left the following day. It was only on July 1, that Mr. James Hope, with Bob, appeared on the stage at the Regal Cinema, Watford — a little surprise initiated by *The Pictorial* — and Mr. Hope received a tumultuous reception."

The announcement of the death of Bob's much-loved "Grandpop Hope" from the *The Hitchin Pictorial* of 27 July 1943.

6
The Art of Scientific Cracksmanship

Bob Hope's unique style of comedy is the result of his own hard work and dedication to the highly skilled art of making the public laugh, as well as from the inspiration he received from several famous predecessors in show business. Although as recently as 1979, he told one interviewer, Brooks Riley, "I was probably influenced subconsciously by all my predecessors — I think comics are," the truth of his success cannot be so easily generalised. And in studying his long and eventful career it is possible to discover the influence upon him of a specific group of stage and screen personalities: in particular the pioneer movie stars Wallace Reid, Charlie Chaplin, Charlie Chase and Raymond Griffith, and the stage comedians Frank Fey, Sid Field and Jack Benny.

Like many others in his profession, Bob was first attracted to comedy in the audience seats of the local cinemas and theatres in the Cleveland neighbourhood where he grew up. And though money was always short during these years, his mother's generosity, or alternatively some hard-earned pocket money, provided the passport to these semi-darkened worlds where one day he himself would become a major star.

The earliest silent screen star that Bob recalls watching was the tragic figure of Wallace Reid (1891–1923) who delighted

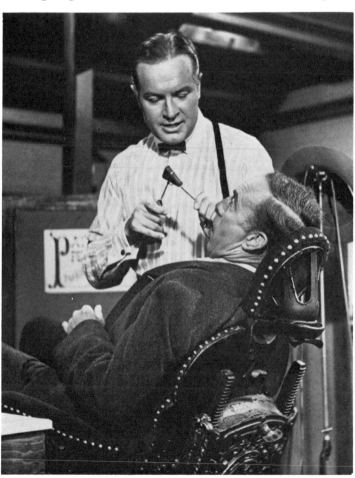

There's more than one way to extract a laugh! Bob playing a dentist, Painless Peter Potter, in one of his most popular films, *The Paleface* (1948).

Film comedian Wallace Reid: "Man, he was *it*!"

The Ghostbreakers — the Wallace Reid film which Bob remade in 1940.

audiences with character parts in some of the earliest comedies he made for the Selig Company, such as *The Reporter* (1911) and *Chumps* (1912). Reid went on to become a leading man as well as a director of such widely popular three-reel movies as *The Quack* (1914) and *A Yankee From The West* (1915). Perhaps his most famous appearance, though, was in D. W. Griffith's classic, *The Birth of a Nation*, made in 1915.

Wallace Reid was equally adept at playing character parts as he was resolute heroes, but then in 1919 when his popularity was at its peak, he was injured in a train accident and began taking morphine to ease his pain. Addiction to this drug, coupled with increasing drinking, led to an agonising death in a sanatorium when he was just 32.

This sad end to Reid's career was, however, years away when the youthful Bob Hope began watching his movies in Cleveland — movies that the comedian-to-be never forgot. Writing in 1954, Bob said: "I used to go to the cheap cinemas and watch Wally Reid. Man, he was it! He used to jump into his low-cut speedster with the top down and then stop his car and jump out. I tried it in a Model-T Ford and almost broke my leg, it was such a long way to the ground!"

By a curious coincidence, one of Wallace Reid's last films was a haunted house farce, *The Ghostbreakers*, which he made in 1922. In 1940, a remake of this self-same story by Paramount with Bob in a leading role was to help confirm his popularity as a star of the screen!

A bigger influence still was unquestionably Charlie Chaplin, whose meteoric rise to fame began in 1914. Talking to Brooks

FOUR MORE DAYS LEFT FOR CHAPLIN CONTEST

By this time all of you who have applied must have your back copies of last week's Evening Journal for the Charlie Chaplin contest. You have until Saturday midnight to send them in—four more days.

You can thank the extraordinary erly assembled, on a blank sheet success of the contest for your of paper so that they form a com-

Bob was also a great admirer of Charlie Chaplin and actually won a contest impersonating the "Little Tramp" in 1914. Almost 70 years later, in 1981, Bob was delighted to receive the Charles Chaplin Award for excellence in the art of film in Los Angeles.

Riley, Bob confided, "I loved Chaplin, and started imitating him when I was a kid. I couldn't do him, though."

In fact, this depreciation by Bob of his skill at mimicry somewhat contradicts what he had said earlier — but whether the statement is true or not, he certainly *did* get his first taste of show business imitating the little tramp in a talent contest held in Cleveland in 1914 when Bob was 10. Writing in the *Sunday Graphic* in 1954, he said:

"Charlie Chaplin imitations first made me show-business conscious. I'd put on my Chaplin make-up and walk duck-legged to the corner past the Fire Brigade House, twirling a rattan cane and flapping a pair of oversize, battered shoes. Amateur Charlie Chaplin contests had broken out in the country's theatres like a rash, and I was so good at it that I was persuaded to enter a contest in Luna Park."

At this point in his narrative, what sounds like the irrepressible joker in Hope takes over and we must judge the rest of this particular tale as best we can. "To make sure I won," Bob goes on, "my brothers rounded up all the neighbourhood kids and took them along to applaud. The man running the contest held his hand over my head, the noise sounded like Indians screeching around a wagon train. The result was a new cooking stove for Mom. It was the first prize!"

Another influence on young Bob was a comic who had co-starred with Chaplin in several of his early Keystone movies. This was Charlie Chase (1893–1940) who, like Chaplin, had graduated into films via musical comedy and vaudeville. In time, Chase not only starred in, but also directed, many of his own movies and became widely popular playing either meek little men hen-pecked by their wives or

Movie comic Charlie Chase: "Some of his pictures were as good as Charlie Chaplin's."

dapper but rather shy fellows always running into unexpected problems. He also made a memorable appearance with Laurel and Hardy in their classic movie, *Sons of the Desert* (1933).

Chase, unlike many of his contemporaries, successfully made the transition to sound films, thanks to his excellent speaking and singing voice, but sadly like the ill-fated Wallace Reid took to the bottle and died of a heart attack, aged 46.

"Charlie Chase was a marvellous comic," says Bob. "He was so good at making the audience aware that trouble was about to hit him before he knew it himself. Some of the best of his pictures are as good as Chaplin's."

Raymond Griffith (1890–1957), the fourth of Bob's screen influences, came from a show business family and after a career as both actor and screenwriter, predominantly associated with comedy pictures, became a producer for 20th Century Fox. Bob remembers Griffith's hilarious silent debut

Screen comedian Raymond Griffith: "A marvellous comic — I'd rate him with Buster Keaton and Harry Langdon."

in *A Scoundrel's Toll* made in 1916, and this was followed by other gems such as *Fools First* (1922), *Changing Husbands* (1924) and *Wet Paint* (1926). His last appearance on the screen was also to prove his most famous — as the dying French soldier in the First World War classic, *All Quiet On The Western Front* (1930).

"Raymond Griffith was another marvelous comic," says Bob. "I'd rate him with Buster Keaton and Harry Langdon, both of whom I also loved. But I never tried to copy any of them — though I think you subsconsciously pick things up. If you hang around with somebody all the time that does certain things to you — you find yourself aping them a little. But I never really tried to copy anybody."

Just as Bob found stars to admire on the cinema screen, so there were entertainers he saw in the flesh in the theatres who fired his youthful enthusiasm. In this context, Bob is quick to pick out the versatile Frank Fey (1873–1938) as a major influence. "He was one of my dear favourites. My God, he was a fantastic timer of comedy," Bob commented in 1979.

In two interviews, Bob has talked about this lugubrious comic who was one of the most popular American vaudeville stars for almost a quarter of a century, but is now little remembered. In the first of these, with Timothy White of *Rolling Stone*, he revealed how he had first been introduced to the theatre by his mother. She had always been fond of live entertainment and it was her enthusiasm that resulted in Bob's memorable first encounter with Frank Fay.

"My father worked all the time, but my mother always found time and affection for me, and when I was quite small she started taking me to the vaudeville shows at Keith's Theatre on 105th Street in Cleveland. One time we went to see this great comedian called Frank Fey. In the middle of his act, my mother said in a loud voice that you could hear in the balcony, 'He's not *half* as good as you!' Everybody turned around, and I actually slid off my seat."

For a youngster who had only one slightly dubious win in a Chaplin look-alike contest and some home entertaining to his credit, one can well appreciate Bob's embarrassment at this moment! But it was to prove the beginning of his admiration for Frank Fey — and the first of many times he saw him in performance.

In the second interview, with Michael Wale of *The Times*, he talked about how he had developed his stage craft — and the debt he owed to Frank Fey.

"I was influenced by guys like Frank Fey. He was the sharpest I've ever seen in working to an audience. I can't work as slow as he was. He would economise on material so much by slowing everything down. He'd get a laugh just on the mood and motions. I remember once at the Palace, Chicago, he was in a spotlight and there was a piano on the stage and somebody sitting at it. He was very grand, what you'd call a distinguished bum. 'Tonight,' he said, 'I'm

Vaudeville star Frank Fey: "He was one of my favourites — a fantastic timer of comedy."

British-born comedian Sid Field, another star Bob greatly admired, playing a difficult tree shot! His partner is another well-known English actor, Jack Warner.

going to play the piano.' And he walked very slowly over to the piano, saw someone was there, and walked very slowly back to the front centre of the stage again and just said, 'There's somebody there'. That was all and the place broke apart."

It was, of course, in Chicago that Bob made his debut later as a stage comic . . .

Another of his comedy heroes was, in fact, British-born. He was the sad-faced comic Sid Field (1904–1950) who was born in Edgbaston on the singularly appropriate date for a person destined for his profession — April Fool's Day! Though highly popular on the British music halls from 1916, Sid's three excursions into films (*That's The Ticket*, 1940; *London Town*, 1946; and *Cardboard Cavalier*, 1947) were not successful at the box office, mainly due to poor scripts that made little use of the star's comic talents. Bob, though, was full of admiration for Field whom he actually first saw on a war-time

Jack Benny: "A lot of comedians can milk a joke — but he could get chicken fat out of it!"

return visit to England. He recalled in a 1970 interview:

"One of the finest comedians I ever watched work was Sid Field. I saw him first in London in 1943. Of course he came out of vaudeville and it's a great pity for comedy that it's died. When I was starting I worked little tab shows in little towns. I had 10 solid years working every kind of audience so that when I finally arrived at Broadway and I was at a rehearsal and Jerome Kern said, 'How the hell did you get this ease on the stage?' I replied, 'Mr. Kern, you don't know what I've been through.' I can just imagine Sid Field might have said that at some time, too!"

The last of Bob's influences probably needs very little introduction — because for years Bob used him as the butt of many of his jokes, building up an impression that the two men must be great rivals. He was the radio and TV comedian Jack Benny (1894–1974), and in fact the men were great friends.

Bob, indeed, has more than once spoken of his admiration for Benny's great ability as a timer of comedy.

"No one had Jack Benny's timing," he told an interviewer in New York in 1986. "A lot of comedians can milk a joke — but he could get chicken fat out of it."

During the years when Jack was alive, Bob told many jokes about his friend's apparent inability to play the violin he invariably carried under his arm (Benny had actually started out in show business as a violinist), and his reputation as a miser. "In fact, the biggest file in my library of jokes is about Jack Benny," Bob said to another journalist in 1971, going on to quote just two of the hundreds of barbed comments he had made about his friend. "Comedians are very cruel to Jack. They say things like they saw him using a ladder to climb into a pay lavatory, when they should know he always crawls under the door. I met him recently. He was swimming under a toll bridge. We met head on!"

In introducing himself this way into the joke, Bob provides a glimmer of the respect and affection in which he always held Jack Benny. The same respect, in fact, that he has for all the other comedians that have been mentioned and to whom he has also acknowledged a debt. That he can be numbered among them is not something he might claim — or certainly not without a huge grin — but is certainly an accolade his friends and admirers would undoubtedly award him.

For Bob Hope has surely now perfected 'The Art of Scientific Cracksmanship' to which all great comedians aspire and, in his turn, has inspired a whole new generation of comedians now working this rich vein of fun and laughter which gives the general public such pleasure.

"Travelling Hope-fully" 7: Some rough travelling for Bob and Jerry in the Marshall Islands.

7
I
And
Crosby

Bing Crosby, the young crooner, at
the time he first met Bob Hope.

Bob's partnership with Bing Crosby is one of the show business legends of the twentieth century, familiar throughout the world and still kept alive by the reshowing of the films they made together. The pairing of these two very different but compatible personalities first occurred on the stage, graduated to radio and then became world-famous in films. In May 1948, Bob wrote the following typically idiosyncratic article about his friend for the leading US movie magazine *Photoplay*, and it is here returned to print for the first time in 40 years!

If I were a man given to phrases, instead of the other way 'round, I'd call this a soul test. Now that I've thought about it, I will call it a soul test.

Imagine *Photoplay* asking one great actor to talk about another great actor.

Favorably, that is.

Yet *Photoplay* requested that I do that very thing. Requested, did I say? They begged. They cried. They finally offered money. I yielded. Not that the money had anything to do with it —no more than fangs have to do with a wolf's jaw.

Only after I had consented — me, Bob (Printer's Ink) Hope did they reveal the name of the lad — I mean performer — whom they wished me to estimate. (Get that last hunk of grammar! Sharp, what?)

Crosby, they wanted. Crosby by BOB HOPE. Crosby as HOPE sees him, as HOPE knows him, as HOPE carries him through one "Road" picture after another.

I and Crosby! Where shall I begin? At the beginning? Well, the only reason I will is because that isn't when you think it was, you cute readers. I and Old Tattered Tonsils may have knit together our first picture *The Road to Singapore* in 1940, but I am wiseing you up to the fact that we worked together six years before that, at the Capitol Theatre in New York.

That is, Crosby worked. Naturally a date like that, to me, was a breeze.

He was young Knucklehead out of the West, at that time. He was an up-and-coming chirp on the canary circuit and he had sidled into pictures (he was, even then, too heavy to come in straight on) by way of a Paramount extravagance called *The Big Broadcast of 1932*.

I, of course, was already famous, my wit the talk of Broadway. I was the dreamboat voted most likely to dock, the Thespian who would restore the Theater to its former grandeur. (How was I to know that a couple of other guys also had the idea of selling popcorn in the lobbies?)

I photographed the Capitol billing during that engagement. "Bing Crosby and Bob Hope" it said, just as it does to this very day in front of your local theater running *The Road to Rio*. (Catch on?)

I took some movie footage on Little Boy Boo-boop-a-Doop at that time, also. He has lived to regret

Bob in one of the more unusual outfits he wore while making *Road to Rio* with Bing in 1947!

that, but I'm sentimental about it and run it frequently for our friends. I love to watch them fall right on their patios watching Cros snapping his fingers, making with the feet and really selling his songs. He gave in those days. Yes, he really did.

In those Capitol days he would stand in the wings and study my work. Thousands had done that before him, of course. It was — it is — the price I pay for my unique style. But one night when I was ambling off after nineteen or thirty encores, Old Tailor's Horror said, "What's with those jokes? The people seem to go for them. Why don't we work up a bit of patter between us to separate my songs?"

I like to help struggling amateurs, so I agreed. We did all right the next matinee. And better the next evening. By the second day we were killing them and we both knew we could be the happiest couple in vaudeville. Or even Hollywood, if we could find the right material.

It was six years before we hit the "Roads" and bussed Lamour. By this time we knew about ourselves and golf; ourselves and families; and more importantly about ourselves and close-ups, which is where we share and share alike, believe you me, Bud.

I have come to realize that Harry Lillis is too smart to give way to temper. He is even too intelligent. (This truth is killing me!) I've always thought that I was a fast study. In fact, I am a fast study. But Bing can walk in the studio, get his lines, give them a quick skim, walk on the set and the scene falls off him, without one cue missing.

You know, don't you, that I have gone mad and am business partners with him and that we share the financing of the "Road" pictures (and those darling little profits) with dear old Paramount? Well, our pictures have more "first takes" in them than any other pictures made in Hollywood. Those looks of astonishment you often see us give one another are not acting. We've had great scripts on those vehicles. Nevertheless, if along in the dialogue, we think of a joke that we think will stump the other one, in it goes while the camera grinds. That way, we will kill each other laughing and we murder Dottie.

He is a natural politician, Bing, but surprisingly, he's no fighter for advantages. I'm the one who goes to the front office and demands that things must be thus and so. Incidentally, one of the things I always insist upon is that I am the funny man. I get the first jokes. Bing is sure to get footage with his cadenzas. The only time I've ever seen him really fight the studio was on *The Road to Rio* when they started to cut out my tight-rope-walking scene. He wouldn't stand for that.

He can be stubborn, and sensitive, and unconcerned, all in one morning. Once we had a big shot at the studio, who announced that we would have no Crosby golf games on Saturday during the shooting of one of our epics. "We will have work instead," he gruffed at us.

"Man, you've had work," said Mr. C. walking right for the door, followed right on his heels by me. We never find out what became of that executive.

This yarn has never been told before, but I think it's one that really shows him up and reveals that quality in him that the camera catches.

During the war we went to Dallas to play a golf match for the benefit of the Red Cross. A guy, whom Bing had known casually in Hollywood as a hoofer and the husband of a star, met us at the train. Now he was an ex-husband and an ex-GI and he explained that he was running a road house, near Dallas. He asked the Throat could he drop by that night and bring me. Bing said okay.

The city officials swooped down on us then, drove us to the links, and a gallery of about 10,000 people. We teed off. About two holes and forty-five minutes later hand bills began fluttering down, all over us. I grabbed one. It said, "Tonight at the Whatnot Inn. Bing Crosby and Bob Hope in Person. Cover charge tonight only, $5.00."

I burned. Handbills like that couldn't be printed so fast.

"Travelling Hope-fully" 8: Jerry Colonna needs a little persuading to leave the beautiful Hawaiian Islands.

Bob unveiling a plaque to commemorate his partner and friend, Bing Crosby, in the London Palladium in March 1979.

The whole routine had to have been planned in advance, the seemingly casual meeting, the seemingly casual request. When the game was over, I hotly told Bing what I thought of it. "Aw, we might as well keep our promise," he said.

So we went over at eight o'clock. From the outside it wasn't a bad trap. The band we heard playing was okay. We made with the entrance, giving out with the teeth and the eager eyes.

There were six people present, at two tables. But the fast manager grabbed us. "Boys, boys, come in," he shouts to the corners, where you could have shot coyotes.

The phone ringing gave us a minute to pick our faces up off the floor. "It isn't really true that Bing and Bob will be there, is it?" a dame asked. Crosby took over. He sang "I Surrender, Dear." She hung up so fast we could practically hear her putting her car into gear, heading our way.

We alternated the calls after that, surrendering dear and thanking for the memory. After auditioning until eleven, we filled up the creep corral. Then we dished them a show till one a.m.

He does like that, my co-star. So I think I'll let him keep on with our double act. He's a really good kid, and while nothing can be done about his taste in clothes or his bad slice in golf, I fully expect that along about 1998 you'll be seeing us wheeling down together on The Road to . . .

8
The Roads
to Success

The seven films which make up what are generically referred to as the "Road" movies have today become justifiably acknowledged as a cult among cinema enthusiasts in general, and among the fans of the three stars, Bing Crosby, Dorothy Lamour and Bob Hope, in particular. According to one estimate, the seven pictures had grossed $50 million dollars by the time the series ended in 1962 (then an all-time box office record) and, since their inception, close to four billion people around the world have seen the films in cinemas or on TV.

As far as Bob is concerned, this remarkable series of zany, exotic and glamorous fantasies full of outrageous humour and in-jokes have also belatedly begun to make critics aware of just what an excellent actor he actually is. In an interview in 1979, Bob spoke of his character in the films as simply "a coward with phoney bravado and all that stuff". Others would rate him and his cinema style rather more significantly than that. Take the British film historian David Pitt, for example, who wrote recently:

"Hope has a deadly accurate eye for the foibles of his character . . . Like all great classic comedians, Hope rarely makes an unfair bid for the audience's sympathy. Considered dispassionately, the character he plays is usually rather despicable. Inordinately vain, a seedy shyster who runs at the first hint of danger, who definitely has his price and is quite prepared to double-cross anyone, regardless of sex and age, to save his skin. But it is precisely because he *is* uncompromisingly all these things that he does endear himself. As with Will Hay and W. C. Fields, his targets are pretension, deceit and hypocrisy. When we laugh at Hope, we laugh at the worst in ourselves. He is the supreme smart-alec, continually out-smarted."

Another critic, Douglas McVay, has given hearty support to Pitt's words. "Bob Hope," he wrote, "has spent 30 years as one of the screen's devout cowards, lechers, egotists, gourmandisers, fall guys and compulsive wise-crackers: and also as one of celluloid's most commercially successful yet critically neglected funnymen."

The leading American TV chat show host Dick Cavett, an unabashed Hope admirer, has put the case even more strongly: "Every comic thinks of Hope as The King. A much smaller number recognise him as a fine screen performer . . . I can't help wondering how conscious Hope is of how *fine* his movie work is."

Though it was undoubtedly the Road pictures, which he began filming in November 1939, that put Bob on the road to stardom, he had already demonstrated his own intrinsic acting style in the first of his major pictures, the haunted house comedy *The Cat and the Canary*, which he had made earlier that same year with Chaplin's former leading lady, Paulette Goddard. Once again, Davit Pitt has not been alone in praising this auspicious screen debut:

"Hope is at his best when playing characters like the hero of *The Cat and the Canary*. The complete craven, the vain, credulous buffoon, the inept con-man with a wry appraisal of his uncomfortable and often dangerous position, winning through with some misguided, desperate spurt of courage."

Successful as this spoof horror picture was — and I, for one, do not even have to see it to be reminded in my mind's eye of one of Bob's best moments when he is asked, "Don't big empty houses scare you?" and he replies, "Not me — I used to be in vaudeville!" to laugh out loud — still, it was in *The Road to Singapore*, released in the spring of 1940 amidst the clamour of war, that international fame at last embraced him.

Interestingly, of all his movie work, Bob remains most fond of the Road pictures. "I see them on TV from time to time," he said not so long ago, "and I'm glad to say they still stand up. They're *still* funny."

Nor does the story end there. For these pictures have also given their title to some of Bob's later special television shows

Dorothy Lamour

Bob Hope

Bing Crosby

Dorothy Lamour — Hollywood Glamour Queen: "It wasn't easy to find an opening when filming with Bob and Bing — but I learned fast!"

(*The Road to China*, etc) as well as being the foundation upon which he built his fortune. We shall be discussing these facts — and the Road pictures which were never made — in the pages which follow, after first tracing the path of this celluloid phenomenon right back to its very beginnings . . .

As with all great success stories, there are varying accounts as to how the Road films were born. One Hollywood legend has it that the series was first planned for the TV favourites, George Burns and Gracie Allen; another that the two comedians Fred MacMurray and Jackie Burns were pencilled in for the production but refused to touch it. (A story which both men have since refuted.)

A third version — almost too good to be true — says the idea was conceived during a game of golf in 1939 between Bob Hope, Bing Crosby and the director, Victor Schertzinger! Apparently Bing and Bob putted out such a string of impromptu gags as they went round the course that they so convulsed Schertzinger he decided to team them up in a picture with Hollywood's latest glamour girl, Dorothy Lamour.

In fact, each of the three stars of the *Road to Singapore* also has a slightly different version of the origins of the series to tell! From such, of course, are myths made — but all are worth the telling.

It seems only right to begin with the lady of the trio, Dorothy Lamour, still hale and hearty and just occasionally filming (she appeared in Stephen King's *Creepshow* in 1988). She lives quietly in North Hollywood and there spoke of her associations with the pictures.

Born in New Orleans in 1914, Dorothy won a beauty contest for "Miss New Orleans" while still in her teens and then became a singer with Herbie Kay's band. It was while she was performing that she was spotted by a talent scout and signed up by Hollywood for what proved dozens of pictures, though, of course, she is best remembered for her appearances in the Road pictures. As a result, she has earned the enduring soubriquet: "The First Lady of the Sarong". This is Dorothy's account of how the Road pictures were born.

"I actually first met Bob Hope when I was singing at a night club in New York. I was appearing with a comedy group called The Yacht Boys who loved to tease me when I was singing, especially if it was a romantic song. They would come on stage, sit down, and then try to break me up by pulling me from one of their laps to another! Bob, who was appearing on Broadway then, was a frequent visitor to the club and laughed at the boys' antics. I've always wondered if that's where he got the idea to have me play 'musical laps' in the Road pictures.

Anyhow, the next time I met Bob was in Hollywood on the Paramount lot. He and Bing Crosby were having lunch, and when I stopped by their table they began to crack jokes at the expense of each other which left me weak from laughing. On my way back to the set where I was working, I met a couple of writer friends and they asked why I was still grinning. I told them I had been joking with Hope and Crosby and that if they could only write a script about two crazy guys and a gal in the middle I would love to be in it.

I think you'll find those two writers have forgotten our conversation that day, but it is a fact that soon after that the first Road story was written and I got my wish to co-star with Bob and Bing."

We now turn to Bing Crosby for his version of what was also to be a turning point in his life. Born Harry Lillis Crosby in Washington in 1904, the young singer came to public notice as a featured vocalist with the Paul Whiteman band. Then, changing his name to Bing after a comic strip called "Bingville Bugle", he became a solo star and radio favourite throughout America in the thirties and forties. In an interview in 1965 he said:

"I first worked with Bob in 1932 at the Capitol Theatre in New York, "but we didn't meet again until I was at Paramount and he'd come along to make some B pictures. For some inexplicable reason he caught on and fast became a favourite!

Then one day someone decided to team us in a picture called *The Road to Singapore*. It was a lucky hunch for everybody involved. The widely publicized Hope-Crosby feud was not a planned vendetta. It was a thing we fell into. It grew out of the fact that when we appeared on each other's radio programmes and in the Road pictures, it seemed easier for our writers to write abusive dialogue than any other kind.

I was intrigued with the idea of working with Bob and Dorothy because it seemed to me that it would be a winning combination. A foreign land, the music, Dorothy in a sarong, Bob being the clown and me singing the ballads — it was one helluva series."

And Bob's 1954 version of the legend-in-the-making:

"After *The Cat and the Canary* which really broke the ice of audience acceptance for me, I went into the first Road picture with Bing. The Road pictures grew out of a typical Hollywood switch: one of those it-starts-out-to-be-this-then-somebody-gets-a-brighter-idea jobs. Originally there was a projected picture called *The Road to Mandalay* and Harlan Thompson was set to be its producer. Who wrote the original version of *The Road to Mandalay* I don't know, but two Paramount contract writers, Frank Butler and Don Hartman, did a rewrite job on it. They changed it from serious to funny and it was retitled *The Road to Singapore*. The name 'Singapore' was used because Don and Frank didn't think 'Mandalay' sounded treacherous enough. As Don put it, 'You take a piece of used chewing gum and flip it at a map. Wherever it sticks you can lay a Road picture, so long as the people there are jokers who cook and eat strangers. If they're nasty and menacing, it'll be a good Road picture. The key to the thing is menace offsetting the humour.'"

According to Bob in a later interview in 1979, he and Bing were brought together as a result of a club appearance they did together which the singer appeared to have forgotten.

"When I got to Hollywood in 1937, I went down to Del Mar to do a show with Bing at The Turf Club. We did a routine that we'd done at the Capitol in New York in 1932. Everybody who saw it — and it played like gangbusters — said, 'Boy, these two guys work well together — let's get a picture for them.' I guess you can say we were feeling each other out in *Road to Singapore*, but then no-one thought it would develop into a series."

In *The Road to Singapore*, Bob plays Ace Lannigan who jumps on board a freighter bound for the East to avoid the enraged father of an old flame, and there meets up with Bing, also running away from an arranged marriage. When they meet up with the beguiling Dorothy, both describe the other as a philanderer in the hope of winning her hand. For what is to prove the first of many times in the series, Bing walks off with the lady's hand.

Bing has recalled how the style which became the hallmark of the pictures — ad-libbing and the occasional in-jokes — was born.

"Travelling Hope-fully" 9: Bob and Jerry hit the jackpot while gambling on a fruit machine in Honolulu.

"That first Road picture quite baffled the director, Victor Schertzinger. Victor was a nice fellow and he'd directed some fine pictures, but he'd had little experience with low comedy. He was a quiet fellow, used to directing his pictures in leisurely fashion. His awakening was rude. For a couple of days when Hope and I tore free-wheeling into a scene, ad-libbing and violating all the accepted rules of movie-making, Schertzinger stole bewildered looks at his script, searching for the lines.

When he couldn't find them he'd be ready to flag us down and say reprovingly, 'Perhaps we'd better do it the way it's written, gentlemen,' then he'd notice that the crew was laughing at our antics. He was smart enough to see that if we evoked that kind of merriment from a hard-boiled gang who'd seen so many pictures they were blasé about them, it might be good to let us do it our way."

If the Hope and Crosby "antics" bemused Victor Schertzinger, it was nothing to what Dorothy Lamour was feeling:

"I had always been very strict with myself about learning my lines. The night before we started *The Road to Singapore*, I naively studied my script like crazy. That was my first mistake. When I arrived on the set, director Victor Schertzinger was already shooting a scene with the two fellows. As I sat and watched, I realised that nothing in their dialogue sounded familiar, not even *vaguely* like the script I'd read. Perhaps there had been some rewrites?

When it was time for my first scene with the boys, ad-libs started flying all over the place. I kept waiting for a cue that never seemed to come, so finally in exasperation I asked, 'Please guys, when can I get *my* line in?' They stopped dead, broke up, and laughed for ten minutes.

It wasn't easy to find the openings, but I learned fast. After the first few days, I decided that it was ridiculous to waste time learning the script. I would read over the next day's work only to get the idea of what was happening!"

Thanks to her sense of humour — which proved an essential ingredient in the success of the series — Dorothy was able to stand her own corner with the two men. The scriptwriters, however, were initially far from amused at the liberties being taken with their work. Says Bob:

"To begin with Don Hartman and Frank Butler didn't like all the ad-libbing because they had written a hell of a good script. And one day when Don walked on the set I yelled, 'If you hear one of your lines, yell Bingo!' Oh, that burned him up and he went to the studio chiefs and complained. But someone said, 'Hey, look at the grosses — and you have your name in big type!' So pretty soon the hostility was gone and he started smiling. I loved the guy. But it was those little touches that Bing and I put in that *made* the pictures. And the audiences were in on it — they *knew* we were fooling around!"

Assisting in all this "fooling around" was Jerry Colonna from Bob's radio show, and Anthony Quinn, who became the first victim of the famous Hope and Crosby "patty cake" routine for escaping from villains. Quinn, who was then himself just starting on the road to fame, has remained forever grateful to the start the series gave him. In a 1975 interview he said:

"Interestingly enough, at that time I was earning extra money hiring myself out to parties for two dollars a night doing imitations of Bing Crosby. So you can imagine how happy I was to get a part! I was one of the few young actors to be allied with Bing and Bob in the Road pictures. I became like a good-luck charm around the studio, because all the pictures that I was in at the time were making such enormous money; and, of course, it was all due to Bing and Bob."

Bob and Bing's "patty-cake" routine in *The Road to Singapore*.

The Road to Singapore was released in April 1940 and was

greeted enthusiastically by the press, rapturously at the box office and ecstatically by the public. What was to prove one of the most successful screen "teams" in film history had been born, a new style of cinema had been evolved, and one of the most lucrative series of movies ever was under way . . .

The success of *The Road to Singapore* clearly demanded a sequel, but according to Bob this came about a year later by another stroke of good fortune:

"Nobody thought that the first Road picture would develop into a series. It became a series when a writer named Sy Bartlett brought in a story called *Find Colonel Fawcett* about two fellows who were trekking through the Madagascar jungles. The catch was that a movie named *Stanley and Livingstone* had just been released and it was so similar to Bartlett's that it ruined it. Bartlett's story was a highly dramatic one, and Don Hartman took it, gagged it up, and named it *The Road to Zanzibar*."

The boys in a tight spot in *The Road to Zanzibar*.

The story features Bing and Bob (playing Fearless Frazier) as two carnival performers in Africa trying to make their way back to America who become involved in a phoney diamond mine and are then conned into "rescuing" Dorothy Lamour from supposed white slavers. Once again Bing scores over Bob in the "I Love Dorothy" stakes.

Victor Schertzinger was hired as the director and wisely decided to let the trio have their heads. "The Road films were the easiest jobs I ever had," the veteran film maker said some years later. "All I had to do was say 'Start' and 'Stop' and then sit back and laugh with the rest of the crew."

This precisely matches Dorothy Lamour's memories:

"The set was as crazy as ever, with wisecracks and ad-libs still flowing like water, but every once in a while I got revenge. During one rehearsal I remained very tight-lipped while Bob and Bing bantered back and forth. The scene ended with them both turning to me and saying, 'How about it?' I smiled demurely and they fell on their faces. Make-up man Harry Ray had blacked out two of my front teeth!"

Dorothy also managed to get more than a look in on the screen by wearing the most eye-catching costumes. Paramount were determined to make as much use of the actress's ravishing beauty as possible (a directive had gone to Schertzinger, "Show as much of Lamour as the censors will permit — with or without sarong!"), and so she was dressed in a skin-tight, flesh-coloured bathing suit to play an apparently nude scene in a bath. On the picture's release in May 1941, this scene resulted in Dorothy being voted one of the "Ten Best Undressed Women" by the Hollywood cameramen! (The film won the 1941 National Board of Review award.)

While making this movie, Bob gave Dorothy the nickname by which she was always known thereafter — "Mommie" — because of her habit of feeling sorry for people down on their luck and finding them jobs.

Bob, who had a memorable scene himself fighting a gorilla, has always rated this particular Road film very highly and believes that under different circumstances it could have earned him an award, too. "I thought I had a chance for an Oscar with *Road to Zanzibar*," he told an interviewer recently in a moment of complete seriousness. "But in those days the academy didn't give much consideration to comedy unless it had some sort of serious thread running through it. Charlie Chaplin and Cary Grant never won Oscars for acting — I keep saying these things to myself!"

What Bob and his co-stars could content themselves with, however, was another well made and hilarious picture which was a huge hit with the public.

The following year brought the third in the series, *The Road to Morocco*, which some critics maintain is the best of them all. The script was once again by Don Hartman and Frank

Opposite:
Dorothy Lamour in her famous sarong. "Show as much of Lamour as the censors will permit — with or without sarong!" Paramount ordered.

The young Anthony Quinn (left) who became "like a good-luck charm" on the Road films, here in a scene from the third of the series, *The Road to Morocco*.

Butler, but with a new director in the person of David Butler.

Bob, who played a vaudeville performer named Turkey Jackson in what is to all intents and purposes a parody of the Hollywood desert epics, remembers this picture for the scenes he played being pampered by some harem lovelies ("Mother told me there'd be moments like this!" he quips) — and being upstaged by a camel:

"The public knows anything can happen in a Road movie, and believe me anything *does* happen. Even the animals can get into a nutsy mood. In one scene we were working with a camel. As I walked up to the camel's head, he turned and spat in my eye! Dave Butler, the director, said, 'Print that. We'll leave it in.' So it was in the finished film — and I can assure anyone who thought it was faked that it *wasn't!*"

Bing Crosby has also recalled that by the time he and Hope made this picture their quick-fire routine of hurling insults at one another had become a byword with the public and both were doing all they could to develop and expand it. In an interview in the late fifties he said:

"Hope is very nimble at this sort of thing, and I can only remember getting the better of him once. That was making *The Road to Morocco* where he gets three wishes from a magic ring and accidentally turns himself into a monkey. When the director, Dave Butler, told me to stand perfectly still so they could match the shot of me with the one of the monkey, I smiled, 'Don't worry, Dave. You're making a monkey out of Ski Nose and you think I won't stand still for that? I'll be a real *statue!*"

Anthony Quinn, who again played the villain in the picture, was told by one of the veteran actors on the set that he was the spitting image of the great silent star, Rudolf Valentino, with whom the old man had actually worked. The result was a special scene in the movie in which Quinn carried Dorothy Lamour, playing Princess Shalmar, off on horseback just as Valentino had done with Agnes Ayres in *The Sheik*.

In the spring of 1944, as the Second World War was moving into its final phase, the all-star team was sent off on the suitably entitled *Road to Utopia*, a picture which Paramount initially intended to be the last in the series. Events, however, were to prove otherwise.

The title of this fourth picture might be said to have been intended to mirror the aspirations of millions of people once the Second World War was over. In fact, it was the first movie in the series to go back in time, to the 1890s, and switch from an exotic location to one that was remote and bitterly cold: Alaska. The script was by Norman Panama and Melvin Frank, and the director was the versatile Hal Walker.

An early scene in the picture indicated that, change of locale notwithstanding, the zany humour was to continue as before. It showed a range of ice-capped mountains and around one of them was the famous semicircle of stars that is the Paramount trade mark!

Crosby and Hope in the famous bar room scene from *The Road to Utopia*.

Again, Bing and Bob are a couple of vaudevillians who this time become involved in the Alaskan gold rush — Bob assuming the name of Chester Hooton — and soon find themselves mistaken for dangerous gunmen who have to battle the climate as well as the wild-life, both human and animal. The two stars had to play what proved an uneasy sequence with a supposedly tame bear (the very day after filming the creature badly savaged its trainer) and an awkward scene on what was supposed to be a glacier, but was actually a high wall in the studio. During filming, the rope which the two stars were hanging onto broke, and Bing landed on top of Bob, damaging his back and causing him pain from which he has never completely recovered.

The film was something of a departure from its predecessors in that it ostensibly allowed Bob to win Dorothy's hand for the one and only time. He also delivered what has since become regarded as one of his classic lines of the entire series. Masquerading as a tough guy in a saloon, he blithely orders a "glass of lemonade" from the bartender, but on seeing the man's menacing glance, adds hastily, "in a *dirty* glass!"

The trio much aged in the final scene of *The Road to Utopia*.

Dorothy Lamour remembers *Utopia* for a different reason:

"Of course, they had to get me into a sarong somehow — even though the temperature was supposed to be 40 degrees below zero! They got round it by having Bob see me coming through the snow all wrapped in furs and then imagining me in a sarong, still holding a fur muff. Believe me that scene wasn't easy to play because the set really was cold and I was afraid for months afterwards that the reviewers would spot my goose bumps!"

In fact, the movie was yet another huge success when it was released in 1945 — one critic declared, "Never has the cult of the he-man been better mocked" — and sheer amazement greeted reports that Paramount were not planning to make any more Road films. Now that peace had been made in the world, it was said, the film-makers felt the public would no longer want such escapist fare. Another report stated that even plans for a highly topical picture entitled *Road To Home*, with Hope and Crosby as a couple of GIs returning from the war to compete for the hand of the girl they had left behind, had been scrapped.

However, the public response was immediate and over-whelming. Paramount received in excess of 75,000 letters from fans demanding that the series continue. Well aware of how successful the pictures had become, Bob now decided a most opportune moment had arrived to negotiate a new and much more favourable deal for the stars. He explains:

"At this time, Bing and I were making around £100,000 a week what with our own radio shows and pictures, but we couldn't save anything because the tax guys grabbed so much. I knew I'd got to work out something so I could take care of my family — keep just a little piece of what I was making from the government. So we went into negotiations with Paramount and after a lot of wrangling we got a deal to finance and produce our own pictures. In time, this meant I wound up with 12 pictures of my own which have proved very valuable."

Just how valuable, Bob has never disclosed, though he admits that he used the money to begin building up the portfolio of investments which have since more than taken care of himself and his family. Among the pictures he owns are, not surprisingly, several of the Road movies which continue to bring him returns whenever they are re-shown on television. "Actually," he says with a grin, "there's a channel in Los Angeles which plays the Road pictures all the time!"

But to go back to the late forties and the fifth picture in the series, *Road to Rio*. Scripted by Edmund Beloin and Jack Rose, and directed by Norman Z. McLeod, the picture took Bob (playing Hot Lips Barton, a carnival musician) and Bing on a colourful journey through the exotic South American land of song and dance to rescue Dorothy from the machina-tions of an evil hypnotist.

Studio publicity photograph for the fifth picture in the series, *The Road to Rio*.

As he now had a financial stake in the series, it is perhaps understandable that Bob's most vivid memories of the picture focus on this new element in their work:

"Before we made *Road to Rio*, Bing and I bought a lot of shares in a soft drink concern, called Lime Cola. We decided to plug this concoction for all we were worth, and we put a big sign advertising it right in the middle of one of the scenes. One of the Paramount officials was down on us like a shot. 'You can't plug a *real* product in a movie,' he said, scandalised. Bing gave him a long, cold look. 'I own a third of this picture,' he said, 'Bob owns another third, and Paramount owns the rest. 'We'll vote for it.'

Strangely enough, the vote resulted in a two-to-one victory for keeping the sign in! But Paramount had the last laugh. By the time the film appeared, that soft-drink business had failed miserably and every time we saw the sign we winced!"

Finance also reared its head for Bob in a quite different way while they were shooting a crowd scene. He recalls:

"We were doing this big scene on a South American set. One day there were 300 visitors on the set in addition to the 200 extras hired for the picture. The electricians spent hours lighting the scene, but when the director called, 'Camera!' the whole place had to be relit. With all those people milling about, things had become so confusing that the electricians had lit the visitors, too!

As partners in the financing, Bing and I put up quite a squawk about the expensive delay. But we soon piped down when it was pointed out to us that 298 of the visitors were our friends or relatives — mostly the latter!"

Nothing, though, could dent their good humour, as one exchange during filming will demonstrate. When Bing kept laughing and ruining a take, Bob suddenly shouted, "This man is crazy — do you realise how much this is costing us?" To which Bing quickly replied, "Sure — but we'll go broke laughing!"

Dorothy Lamour has always been a little resentful that she was never invited to become a partner in the group producing the pictures — as no-one could dispute the importance of her contribution to their success. "The truth is they could have considered a four-way split," she has said, "but no one even asked me. My feelings were hurt, although later they did give me a tiny percentage."

She remembers, too, that Bob could not keep his eyes off the low cleavage of one of the dresses she wore in the picture and this made her fluff her lines several times. Finally, she got her own back by shouting, "Hold everyting a minute while Mr. Hope has a good look!"

It was to be almost five years before Bob got another look at Dorothy Lamour in the sixth picture, *Road to Bali*, which became the first of the series to be shot in Technicolor. Initially, the picture, based on a story by Frank Butler and Harry Tugend, and again directed by Hal Walker, was to be called *Road to Hollywood*, but after considerable rewriting became *Road to Bali* — though the joke was that none of the trio actually reached that fabled island! (Bob actually utilised the first title for a later TV special, as we shall see.) To add to the confusion, Bob and Bing did a routine in kilts with a set of bagpipes and there was a perhaps not-too-serious suggestion that Dorothy should be called Princess MacTavish! (In fact, she became Princess Lalah.)

Bob, who played a song and dance man named Harold Gridley, had a memorable jungle scene which utilised a clip from the classic Humphrey Bogart film, *The African Queen*. After a mirage of the tough guy actor has left behind the Oscar he won for the movie, Bob grabs the little statue from Bing who has picked it up and shouts, "Give me that — *you've* got one!" His scenes trying to avoid being put in a cooking pot by a party of cannibals are also Bob at his most inventive.

In fact, *Road to Bali* contains some of the best scenes that two comedians played together on the screen, a point upon which Bob elaborated in a recent discussion of their relationship:

"Bing and I had a chemistry, there was a thing going on, a mesh thing, where we could talk and stop and look at each other and do little different things that worked so well. We were both lucky enough to be good studies. If you don't rehearse too much, it's so good, because you get such a natural performance. It was also a relief from any of the kind of things we had done on our own. In fact, people said to me that they had no idea that Bing could get that *wild*. But he had it in him — he *loved* it."

Bing totally agreed with this verdict by his partner. "It was like being paid for having fun," he once said simply. Dorothy, though, also recalls this movie because of a scene where Bob and Bing were actually fumbling their lines:

"'Hal!' I called to the director, 'Better warm up Dean Martin and Jerry Lewis — they're not only funnier, but younger!' Everybody laughed except the boys. 'You'd better be careful how you talk to us,' Bob said, 'You can always be replaced by another actress.'"

Although Dorothy had no way of knowing it at the time, those gently sarcastic words were to prove prophetic when the seventh Road picture was being set up in 1961.

The Road to Hong Kong took the company out of Hollywood for the first time, to be filmed at Shepperton Studios in England, with Norman Panama directing a script he had co-written with Melvin Frank. But a bigger surprise still came with the announcement that there was to be no Dorothy Lamour! Gina Lollobrigida or Sophia Loren — it was said — were being tipped for the top female role, although in the end it was a young British actress named Joan Collins (the self-same!) who was presented as Hope and Crosby's new co-star. Lamour, a report said, had been offered a small role but had turned the suggestion down flat. After 21 years with the series, she was just not prepared to play what she saw as a cameo part.

Recently, Dorothy has explained exactly what happened:

"I was certainly hurt when I read about that new Road picture in the papers because no-one had spoken to me about it. Now, because I had been off the screen for a few years I could well understand that they might want a big box office name to star opposite the boys — but under *no*

The Road to Bali, the first Road picture to be filmed in colour, featured Bob and Bing in kilts!

Monkey business! Another hilarious scene from *The Road to Bali*.

Although Joan Collins was to co-star with Bing and Bob in *The Road to Hong Kong*, the public clamoured for Dorothy Lamour and the trio were reunited yet again.

circumstances would I play a bit part! Since all three of us had starred in the Road films, I felt it was humiliating to have my contribution minimalized.

So when they finally asked me to appear I stuck to my guns and said I'd only do it if they built up my part. I realised they all knew it was important I appeared in the movie, and — for a price — I finally did. What was marvellous when I arrived in England was to be met by dozens of journalists and hundreds of fans who followed me everywhere I went. I later heard that both Bob and Bing's secretaries received quite a bit of mail resenting the fact that I was not the girl in the middle. But in the end I was able to forget all the hassle and enjoy working with them both again."

Dorothy was also proud of the fact that without special dieting she wore exactly the same size sarong she had done in the first picture. "Let's face it," she told one journalist, "it wouldn't be a Road film without me in a sarong!"

It remains a fact, that despite the fun the trio once again had filming, this seventh picture was doomed to failure. The storyline was somehow too hackneyed, and though both Bing and Bob (playing yet another song and dance man, Chester Babcock) gave it their best shots, the critics for once were not

A rare picture of Bob and Bing filming one of their comic routines for director Norman Panama on the set of the last of the series, *The Road to Hong Kong*.

impressed and the box office takings proved nowhere near as good as those of its predecessors. As Dorothy Lamour remarked later, "It seemed a terrible end to such a wonderful series."

In fact, as far as Bob Hope was concerned it was *not* to be the end of the road — far from it.

Despite the fact that critical and public appreciation for the picture had not been all that it should have been, that same year the Screen Producers Guild held a "Bob Hope Milestone Dinner" in Hollywood in which show business paid its tribute to the evergreen star. And among the many tributes was one from the President, John F. Kennedy, a committed Road fan. Bob still cherishes the citation given to him on this day, the relevant part of which reads:

"Most Americans are familiar with the Bob Hope movies, *The Road to Morocco*, *The Road to Utopia* and all the other Road shows he has produced. I suppose that after receiving this Award he will seriously consider another — The Road to Washington. I can tell him from my own personal experience that this will not be the easiest road he has ever travelled, but we welcome him on it, and in addition, he would have an opportunity to visit his money — at least what's left of it!"

But the joking aside, in 1977 serious plans were set in motion for another picture, *The Road to the Fountain of Youth*, in which Dorothy Lamour would be asked to appear with Bob and Bing. But, tragically, just as a schedule was being drawn up in October, Bing died suddenly of a heart attack. Could there possibly be a Road picture without him?

The British film impresario Lord Grade, a long-time admirer of the Road movies, believed there could, and when Bob had recovered from the shock of his friend's death, he it was who offered to finance the picture with George Burns as co-star: a choice with which Bob immediately concurred.

Unfortunately, however, other commitments precluded this pairing, and even attempts to get the debonair British comedian, David Niven, to step into the role eventually came to nothing. Bob still, though, nurses the hope that someday *The Road to the Fountain of Youth* might get made.

"It's such a funny idea," he said recently. "It'll use clippings from the earlier Road films to describe the search of these two young gaffers for the secret of youth. I'd still love to do it."

Although, at the time of writing, nothing further of this particular Road movie has been heard, Bob has in the interim appeared in two television shows which have utilised some of the unique elements that made the films so popular.

The first of these, *The Road to China*, was built around a visit he made to that fascinating and mysterious country in 1979. A spectacular four-hour show he gave at the Capital Theatre in Peking was filmed by NBC and extracts were used in *The Road to China* which also showed Bob visiting many of the country's greatest attractions. As ever, his jokes were

Bob in front of the "Democracy Wall" in Peking while filming his TV special *The Road to China* in 1979.

topical — thought it was self-evident his audience didn't understand a word! The show was, though, a first for both Bob and television, as the producer, Jim Lipton, later explained:

"*The Road to China* made Bob the first entertainer to appear in mainland China for American commercial television. As part of the deal for being allowed to film there, I promised the Peking government that Bob would conduct seminars on the side for Chinese comedians and movie and TV people. Talk about ad-libbing! Bob didn't have the vaguest idea of what they were going to ask him, so he just fielded the questions as they came through his translator, Ying Ruocheng. The exchanges were so hilarious that I actually included some of them in the US show."

Among the jokes still remembered with amusement both by viewers and the star himself are these. "The Great Wall? In America it would take 600 years to get a permit to build the Great Wall!" And, "They love Richard Nixon over here — they think Watergate is a rice paddy."

Bob's wife, Dolores, however, who went with her husband on the trip, remembers another story which her husband was not quite so anxious to repeat. "Bob gets upset when people don't recognise him in the street," she told an interviewer on her return. "In China, of course, nobody recognised him because they had never seen him in the movies or anywhere.

Eleven of the leading ladies who have appeared with Bob in films join him on the TV special, *The Road to Hollywood*, in 1983. The ladies are (left to right), Rosemary Clooney, Virginia Mayo, Janis Paige, Jill St.John, Martha Raye, Dorothy Lamour, Lucille Ball, Dina Merrill, Jane Russell, Rhonda Fleming and Martha Hyer.

He brooded. Then one guy came up to him and said, 'Hey — it's Bob Hope!' Bob was overjoyed and chatted with the man for a long time. The only thing was, he turned out be a Chinese-American tourist from San Francisco!"

Most recently of all, memories of the famous series were revived when Bob appeared in a second TV spectacular, *Road to Hollywood*, in March 1983, when clips were shown from each of the seven movies, and numerous guest stars appeared with him to commemorate what was described as "the most successful screen comedy trio of all time". Apart from Dorothy Lamour, some of Bob's co-stars from his other 80-odd films gathered for the celebration including Jane Russell, Jill St. John, Janis Paige, Rosemary Clooney and Lucille Ball.

Bob reminisced nostalgically, "For Bing and Dorothy and me the Road pictures were a romp. There was a great feeling about them. We had fun, the crew making them had fun, and the public had fun. There was a real warmth about them."

If Bob has a regret it was that Crosby always got the girl. But not on *Road to Hollywood* — for the final scene showed him surrounded by all his co-stars, smiling warmly and even a little triumphantly. And as *Time* magazine wrote in applauding the special, "It was the ultimate Road picture — the one in which Hope, now 79, at last got all the girls!"

9

Thrill of my Life

Bob won praise all over the world for his efforts entertaining the troops during the Second World War. The photograph shows him in Britain in 1943, and the newspaper article by the famous American novelist, John Steinbeck, is from the *The Daily Express* of 31 July 1943.

Beginning in May 1941, Bob did the first of what were to prove thousands of special shows for American troops stationed around the world. Initially, he took along the co-stars from his radio shows, comic Jerry Colonna, singer Frances Langford, entertainer Patty Thomas and guitarist Tony Romano — but by the time the war ended other famous show business stars were joining the troupe, including some of the cinema's most famous sex symbols. In the following article, written for the British *Sunday Graphic* in June 1954, Bob talks about his earliest war-time trips and some of the unlikely things that happened.

Flying round a million miles or so in the war, lugging a bag of gags to and fro across the world to amuse Servicemen, I found myself in some pretty odd spots at times.

When I checked in at Bougainville in 1944, for instance . . .

I was having a quick shave before I went in for dinner,

They don't talk about anything else when Bob Hope's coming

by JOHN STEINBECK

WHEN the time for recognition for service to the nation in wartime comes to be considered, Bob Hope should be high on the list.

This man drives himself and is driven. It is impossible to see how he can do so much, can cover so much ground, can work so hard, and can be so effective. He works month after month at a pace that would kill most people.

Moving about the country in camps, airfields, billets, supply depots and hospitals, you hear one thing constantly. Bob Hope is coming, or Bob Hope has been here. The Secretary of War is on an inspection tour, but it is Bob Hope who is expected and remembered.

He gets laughter

IN some way he has caught the soldiers' imagination. He gets laughter wherever he goes from men who need laughter.

He has created a character for himself—that of the man who tries too hard and fails, who boasts and is caught at it.

His wit is caustic, but it is never aimed at people, but at conditions and at ideas. And where he goes men roar with laughter and repeat his cracks for days afterwards.

Hope does four, sometimes five,

shows a day. In some camps the men must come in shifts because they cannot all bear him at the same time.

Then he jumps into a car and rushes to the next place, and because he broadcasts and every one listens to his broadcasts he cannot use the same show more than a few times. He must in the midst of his rushing and playing build new shows constantly.

If he did this for a while and then stopped and took a rest it would be remarkable but he never rests. He has been doing this ever since the war started. His energy is endless.

Hope takes his shows all over. It isn't only to the big camps, in little groups on special duty you hear the same thing. Bob Hope is coming on Thursday. They know weeks in advance that he is coming.

It would be rather a terrible thing if he did not show up. Perhaps that is some of his drive. He has made some kind of contract with himself and with the men and one that no one, least of all Hope, could break.

It is hard to overestimate the importance of this thing and the responsibility involved. The battalion of men who are moving half-tracks from one place to another, doing a job that gets no headlines, no public notice and isn't which must be done if there is to be a victory, are forgotten and they feel forgotten.

A symbol life

THIS writer, not knowing Hope, can only conjecture what goes on inside the man. He has seen horrible things and has survived them with good humour and made them more bearable, but that doesn't happen without pain.

He is cut off from rest and even from admitting weariness. Having become a symbol he must lead a symbol life.

Probably the most difficult, the most tearing thing of all is to be funny in a hospital. The long low buildings are dispersed in case they should be attacked. Working in the gardens or

reading in the lounge rooms are the ambulatory cases in maroon bathrobes. But in the wards in the long aisles of pain the men lie with big eyes turned inward on themselves and on their people.

Some are convalescent with all the pain and itch of convalescence. Some work their fingers slowly, and some cling to the little trapezes which help them to move in bed.

Everything that can be done is done but medicine cannot get at the lonesomeness and the weakness of men who have been strong. And nursing cannot shorten one single endless day in a hospital bed.

And Bob Hope and his company must come into this quiet inward and lonesome place and gently pull the minds outward and catch the interest and finally bring laughter up out of the black water. There is a job.

It hurts many of the men to laugh, hurts knitting bones, strains at sutured incisions, and yet laughter is a great medicine.

Once in hospital . . .

THIS story is told in one of those nameless hospitals which must be kept safe from bombs.

Hope and company had worked and gradually they had got the leaden eyes to sparkling, and

planted and nurtured and coaxed laughter to life.

A gunner who had a stomach wound was gasping softly with laughter. A railroad casualty slapped the cast on his left hand with his right hand by way of applause. And once the laughter was alive the men laughed before the punch line, and it had to be repeated so they could laugh again.

Finally it came time for Frances Langford to sing. The men asked for As Time Goes By.

Her voice is a little hoarse and strained. She has been working too hard and too long. She got through eight bars when a boy with a head wound began to cry.

There is a man

SHE stopped and then went on, but her voice wouldn't work any more, and she finished the song whispering, and then she walked out as no one could see her, and broke down.

The ward was quiet and no one applauded. And then Hope said into the aisle between the beds and he said seriously, "Fellows, the folks at home are having a terrible time about you. They can't get any powder eggs at all. They've got to use the old-fashioned kind that you break open."

There's a man for you—there is really a man.

WORLD COPYRIGHT.

just after we arrived, when the sudden thunder of heavy guns 200 yards away nearly knocked me flat. Our fellows were still fighting off Jap counter-attacks against our base on the island.

I finished my shave with a pretty shaky hand, and was still shaky thinking of lurking Japs when I left my shack and walked along the dark path to General Griswold's mess-hut.

SHADOW-BOXING

I was busy dodging shadows when suddenly somebody caught me a crack across the head from behind. I hit out and wrestled like a madman, and then suddenly realised that what I was wrestling with had leaves, not hands. I'd stepped on the end of a broken branch, and it had come up and hit me.

That same year I was in Banika in the South-west Pacific. A Special Service Marine officer came over.

"We've got the First Marine Division stashed on a little island called Pavavu, training for the invasion of Pelelieu. They haven't had any entertainment for months. Will you go over with your troupe?"

"We'll be ready tomorrow morning," I said. I knew I had no need to ask my gang. Frances Langford, Jerry Colonna, Patty Thomas and the rest of them had never turned down a show.

We flew in tiny Cub planes, for there were no runways and we had to land on the road.

When we reached Pavavu, more than 15,000 guys were standing waiting for us.

As we flew over, they all let out a yell. It felt as if our little planes were being lifted right up in the air on that yell.

We did a show for them, and when we got into the Cubs to go back to Banika, all 15,000 of those Marines lined both sides of the road and cheered as each of us took off.

If I never get another thrill in my life, that one will last me.

HAPPY DAYS

You can pull down 20,000 dollars for a single show — *but if the audience doesn't like you, you won't be happy.*

But if you work an audience for nothing and you're a hit and you feel that old electricity crackling back and forth between you and the people as we used to in those old shows-for-the-Services days — then you're happy, and being there is really worthwhile.

10

You Should Have Heard the Pins Drop!

Comedian Jerry Colonna — as seen by cartoonist Sig Vogt.

Jerry Colonna, the unmistakable American comic with his walrus moustache and bulging eyes, was for years one of Bob's most consistent co-stars as well as closest friends. It was on Hope's radio shows that "Professor" Colonna — as he was known — with his piercing voice, became a national favourite, and he later appeared with Bob in numerous films and on television. During the first wartime trips to entertain the servicemen, Jerry kept a diary of the troupe's exploits and later recounted these in a style as zany and full of wise-cracks as anything Hope might have written. The following report describes a visit to tiny Majuro Island in the Pacific in July 1944 on a tour that took the party from San Francisco through Hawaii, on to dozens of small islands, and then to New Guinea and Australia. (When Jerry Colonna later fell ill, Bob was generous in his help for his old friend, who died in November 1986.)

Flying from Makin to Majuro that morning I felt in a meditative mood. What was it that had brought me all the way from a humble Boston schoolboy to this great job of travelling all over the world to entertain our fighting men? There were just two words that could answer it—*fight and work*. All my life I have fought work. It is surprising how often I have won.

All of a sudden both of my ears popped. It meant the "Seventh Heaven" was sitting down on the island of Majuro. How did I know this? Was it clairvoyance? Was it some jungle instinct I had developed? Or was it the pilot yelling, "We're sitting down on Majuro Island!"

He really knew how to fly that plane. They say a good pilot flies by the seat of his pants. He was so good he had worn out four pairs.

A native delegation met us at the plane. They were led by a very old white man. He seemed to be their king. Some of the men on the island said he was a descendant of Captain Christian of "Mutiny On The Bounty" fame. I couldn't believe this. He didn't resemble Clark Gable at all.

I wondered how it must feel to be a ruler. Then my thoughts soared higher. I wondered how it must feel to be a yard stick. I know that if I were in this man's place, if I were leader of a thousand ferocious natives, there is one thing I would certainly do. I would get out of there as soon as possible!

Hope took one look at the natives and said, "It looks like I'm on location for another one of my Road pictures!" Then he glanced at the old king and said, "My! hasn't Crosby aged!"

I tried to be friendly with the natives, but I just couldn't understand a word they were talking about. I didn't know enough about the Brooklyn Dodgers.

The ancient white man gave a signal to his followers and they began an island dance to the accompaniment of the tom-toms. I asked the old man where these strange primitive rhythms came from. He told me they came from a far away country, which, in their tongue, was called "The Palladium."

When the natives had finished putting on their show for us, we decided the least we could do was return the compliment. It seems I had swiped a compliment when they weren't looking. Although they hadn't asked us to, we went ahead and gave our show for them.

Hope started off with his usual monologue. For ten minutes he told jokes, and for ten minutes there was a deafening silence.

Bravely he continued.

Once he stopped cold. He thought he heard a chuckle from the back row. He listened. It was only a bull frog calling to his mate.

Again Hope turned to us and in a funereal voice muttered, "If this whole island were a frying pan, it wouldn't be big enough to hold the omelet I'm producing today."

A Naval officer explained to him that the natives didn't laugh because they didn't understand. Then Patty came out and did her dance. The natives smiled. They understood.

When Frances sang, the native faces broke into broad grins. Great, I thought. At last the show was going over.

Bob and Jerry Colonna on stage together — a sight recalled with affection by millions.

Bob's unhappy experience on the beach as cartooned by Sig Vogt.

But then we discovered the true reason for their smiles. They thought we were auctioning off the girls.

One other time we had a similar experience with an audience that didn't understand. During our Caribbean trip, a group of Puerto Rican soldiers asked Hope to give a show for them. They couldn't understand a word of English and he couldn't understand a half word of Spanish.

Hope's monologue proceeded in the following manner: Joke, no laugh; joke, no laugh; big joke, big no laugh! Hope was desperate. He wrung his hands, but still no laugh. The Puerto Ricans' faces looked like they were all in straight-jackets. Finally Hope signed off with, "Que Pasa?" which means in Spanish, "How goes it?" This brought down the house. The soldiers were so happy to learn that Bob Hope spoke Spanish.

I followed Hope on the stage and as I appeared, there was a tremendous ovation. I opened my mouth. They cheered for ten minutes. I closed my mouth. How could I top that? I was puzzled. Even that brought applause. They pointed at me, looked at each other, laughed and yelled, "Bigotte! Bigotte grande!" We were unable to go on with the show until we found out what I had done to inspire such a commotion. It turned out that I looked exactly like the Governor of the Island. He wore a big mustache (Bigotte grande) which was the duplicate of mine.

Hope said, "from now on, Colonna, watch your step. I've finally found a guy who can replace you."

"Okeh," I said, "then *I* can be the governor of Puerto Rico!"

A shot rang out. The Revolution had started.

But getting back to Majuro (and I'm glad we are), we did three shows on the island, entertaining 4500 soldiers.

For relaxation we went swimming in the ocean. Here the water is very warm, and so clear you can see the bottom. I looked down and there I could see a little black crab nipping at my toes. Egad! what am I standing here for?

I'll tell you what I was standing there for. There was a beautiful Army nurse swimming five yards away. Hope tried to make an impression by swimming way out from the shore by himself, when suddenly he set up a terrific thrashing and splashing in the water.

We sat around the beach watching him and wondering idly whether or not there would be any life insurance. At last we got our answer. A minute or two later he came walking up the sand dragging a dead octopus. The nurse wasn't the least bit impressed and walked away. Hope, dejected, unscrewed the cap and let the air out of the octopus.

All in all it was one of the pleasantest afternoons of our trip. Tony brought his guitar along. We were entertaining some Seabees when Frances and Patty appeared in their bathing suits. Two hours later Bob came by and dug our trampled bodies out of the sand. Hope told the girls to yell "Fore!" from now on before they walked by.

11
Bob and the Beauties

Some of the most famous sex symbols of recent times have accompanied Bob on his 25 Christmas shows to entertain American servicemen around the world, which became a tradition for almost a quarter of a century until the last one in 1972. Most of these lovely ladies remember their tours with pleasure, their affection for Bob and the shows having survived often extremely inhospitable climates and occasionally dangerous situations. From Greenland to Vietnam, and from the Caribbean to the Far East, the Bob Hope Christmas Shows took gags and girls to where the action was, and earned their star the admiration of millions of servicemen who were a long way from home. The reminiscences of these girls begin with those of Anita Ekberg, who appeared with Bob in the very first of these shows to be filmed for television in 1954.

Bob with the Swedish-born star Ann-Margaret, one of his favourites among the lovely ladies who have accompanied him on his Christmas trips overseas to entertain US troops.

Anita Ekberg

The blonde Swedish sex symbol of the fifties and sixties, actually owes her break in show business to Bob Hope. "I suppose it was rather appropriate for someone who had been labelled 'The Iceberg' to get started in Greenland — but that's what happened to me," says Anita, who first came to America in 1951 as "Miss Sweden" to take part in the Miss Universe contest and was later the subject of five pages of pictures in *Esquire* magazine under the headline, "Ekberg, the Swedish Iceberg". "I did a lot of modelling and appeared on the covers of all sorts of pin-up magazines. I met Bob just before Christmas 1954. He was about to go to Thule Air Base in Greenland to do his Christmas Show for the troops. Apparently, Marilyn Monroe was going to be his co-star but she cancelled out at the last moment. Bob asked me if I would like to go in her place."

The show was to be the first to be televised and it obviously presented Anita with a unique opportunity — and coming from Malmo in Sweden which often has sub-zero temperatures in the winter, the thought of going to Greenland in mid-December did not deter her whatsoever. She was under no illusions, however, that it was her statuesque figure — 39 inch bust, 23 inch waist and 37 inch hips — which was what had attracted Bob to her for she had very little acting experience: a fact the comedian himself has readily admitted.

"I had just heard from Marilyn's husband, Joe DiMaggio, that she was ill and couldn't go with us. That night I was emcee at a football banquet in Los Angeles, and among the guests was this beauty contest winner wearing a sweater with UCLA on it. The U and the L were outstanding! Although she was virtually unknown at the time, Anita was strikingly beautiful and unbelievably stacked. Right then and there I invited her to come to Thule."

Anita also remembers the conversation vividly. "He asked me where I was from. 'Sweden', I said. 'What are you doing for Christmas?' he went on. For just a moment I wondered if he was propositioning me. 'I'm going to Detroit' I think I replied. 'No you're not,' he said firmly. 'You're coming with me to Greenland and I'll pay you $2,500.'"

Her delight at the opportunity apart, Anita was still able to be philosophic about the reason why it had been offered. Speaking not long after returning from the tour; she said:

"If a girl has a beautiful bust she should not go around covered up. I don't mean she should go around naked to the waist, but she should not be completely hidden. In Sweden the body has always been considered beautiful. And I like it when men look at me in the street — you can hear their shoes grind on the sidewalk when they turn around!"

And *did* she turn the heads of the servicemen in Greenland! As Bob himself has recalled, "When she came on stage in a fur coat, three thousand men stood up, applauded, whistled and

Anita Ekberg: "She had a cleavage that made the Grand Canyon look trivial."

cheered. Then she took off the coat and stood there in a low-cut gown which showed cleavage that made the Grand Canyon look trivial. It was bedlam!"

Anita remembers the show, too. "The boys really gave us a wonderful reception. The show was the first to be televised and it got one of the highest ratings for the Christmas season. Hedda Hopper, the newspaper columnist, was on the tour and gave me some wonderful publicity. Thanks to that invitation from Bob, everyone was after me for TV and films when we got back to the States."

Interestingly, Anita's first picture was called *Blood Alley* in which she played a young Chinese girl complete with black wig and ragged clothes! Soon afterwards, though, it was the spectacular Ekberg figure which had caught Bob Hope's eye that was being exploited to the full in the 25–odd films she subsequently made. Now living in Rome, Anita recalls:

"It was some years before I saw Bob again and then he joked that he hadn't been able to use me because my fee had gone up to $75,000! But I did work with him in 1963 when we made *Call Me Bwana* at Pinewood Studios in England. He hadn't changed much: the same demon for work, funny and warm as well. I have a lot of admiration for him — even if he doesn't like paying repeat fees!"

Bob, too, has retained a soft spot for Anita Ekberg, and in an interview a few years back, actually replied to a journalist's question as to which of all the sex symbols he had worked with was his favourite, by telling the story of how he first met Anita . . .

Jayne Mansfield

Once described by *Life* magazine as "Broadway's smartest dumb blonde", Jayne was the star attraction of Bob's first tour to the Far East in 1957. Alternately referred to as the "bosomy sexpot of Hollywood", Jayne had risen to international fame through beauty contests, some stage and TV appearances, and then a starring role in the rock'n'roll picture, *The Girl Can't Help It* in 1957. Such was Jayne's success on Bob's Christmas Shows that she made a total of three tours with him before her tragic death in a car accident in 1967. Jayne told one reporter after returning from the first tour in 1957:

"Appearing with Bob has made me want to play in comedy because he is such a master. In fact the whole tour was a great experience for me — especially our stopover in Okinawa. There I became the first American movie star to make a personal appearance in one of their picture theatres and over a thousand people turned out. You never saw such a crowd. Bob also introduced me to a man called Kotara Kokuba, who he said was the richest man in Okinawa. Apparently he was so pleased with my appearance at the theatre he threw a feast for us afterwards at one of his teahouses!"

Like her predecessor, Anita Ekberg, Jayne was well aware that it was her amazing 41 inch bust, tiny 21 inch waist and 35 inch hips that drove the servicemen wild — that, and the revealing clothes she invariably wore. Yet Bob has always been unstinting in his praise for the dizzy blonde.

"Make no mistake about it, Jayne was a real trouper. She never complained about anything — and believe me there were times when there was plenty to complain about. For instance, before each stop she had to change into a new costume. And this meant squeezing into the tiny lavatories they have on aeroplanes — no mean feat.

Wherever Jayne appeared the guys went crazy. I remember when she appeared on stage in Hawaii so many

flashbulbs went off I thought Pearl Harbor was exploding all over again! For five minutes solid they popped away with their cameras while I tried to get the routine with Jayne started. Even when we *did* start I knew I didn't have the guys' attention: she was one hell of an act to follow."

Jayne herself explained her success quite matter-of-factly, "I've just got a body that is big. If they want me to exploit sex, I'll exploit sex. But I know it can't last forever" — a tragically apt remark, as time was to prove.

The tour also took Bob and Jayne to Japan, where they played an uproariously popular spy sketch for the men of the Tachikawa air base. Jayne was a seductive spy and Bob an impressionable serviceman.

"I was cast as a Mata Hari type and Bob was this security risk about to go on leave," Jayne recalled later. "All the guys appreciated what a state Bob was in — and Bob enjoyed it too!"

In 1959, Jayne was reunited with Bob a second time for the Christmas Show in Alaska — a very far cry from the heart of the Far East — but again Jayne dazzled her audiences with her skimpy clothes. She explained to pressmen: "Most women wear too many clothes. I feel great all the time wherever I am because I know there's just me and the dress. I have never owned a bra and a girdle, and I haven't worn stockings since I was weaned. And even being in Alaska wasn't going to change all that!"

Jayne also got herself some tremendous publicity by arranging to have a lion cub waiting for her when she landed at Anchorage. The photographs of her posing with the cub while Bob stood rather nervously behind made the front pages of newspapers all over the world. Another member of the company who also kept a very wary eye on the lion was a young actor named Steve McQueen!

There is an interesting sequel to this story. Some years later, when Jayne was invited to appear at a charity ball in the Beverly Hilton Hotel in Hollywood, which was being hosted by Bob, two equally bosomy young starlets did their best to upstage her by hanging on to each of the comedian's arms, thereby leaving her standing on the side. But, without a moment's hesitation, she stepped up to the microphone and asked the audience, "Would you like to hear Bob and I sing a song that we sang together for our boys in Alaska?" The response was instant and defeaning — and Jayne was able to allow herself a smile of satisfaction as Bob extricated himself from the dismayed starlets and joined her. And as the pair began to sing, the girls had no choice but to slink embarrassedly from the stage!

"Behind that amazing superstructure lurks a very clever woman," Bob told reporters when he and Jayne were on their third tour, to Newfoundland, in 1961. "Mind you, she can start an avalanche by just bowing. I asked one of our audiences, 'Would you like to hear Jayne sing?' and this G.I.

shouted, 'We just like to see her breathe!'"

Jayne always remembered this particular tour for an unintentional *faux-pax* she made. "I was introduced to these Royal Canadian Mounted Police — you know, the ones in the bright red jackets. Without stopping to think, I said, 'I didn't know you were real. I thought you were just in the funny papers.' They took it very well, though!" she said.

Another memorable incident occurred when Jayne telephoned Bob one evening in a panic to tell him that she had lost one of her earrings in the snow. The comedian told her there was no way she would find it in the dark and better to leave any search until the morning. A few minutes later, however, he happened to glance out of his window and see literally hundreds of servicemen with torches obviously intent on finding the missing earring. She had obviously called for help from the servicemen. As a matter of fact, no one found the earring — for Jayne had mistakenly put both of them on the same ear!

Bob's most enduring memory of all of the trips he made with Jayne was when she sang a beautiful version of "White Christmas" — winning the hearts of thousands of men who until that moment had only thought of her as a dumb, stacked blonde. Following her sad death, Bob penned this tribute:

"Jayne made three Christmas trips with us and appeared on many of our shows. She was always a delight — the audiences loved her, the other members of the cast loved her. She had a fantastic style. I could never quite figure her out, though. One moment she was the most naive little girl in the world and the next minute you had the feeling she was putting the whole world on. You know she had a swimming pool in her home that was coloured pink and shaped like a heart? Well, that was Jayne, too — pink and heart-shaped. I really miss her."

Gina Lollobrigida

Gina was to be the star feature of Bob's mammoth 1958 Christmas tour which took in seven countries, including the Azores, North Africa, Europe and Iceland. Although "La Lolla", the Italian carpenter's daughter who had graduated into films via modelling for illustrated novels, was already one of Europe's most famous sex symbols, at this time, she had only just started to make an impact on American movie-goers when she and Bob first appeared together in Madrid.

"Actually, I had met Bob Hope a few years earlier during one of his trips to Europe," Gina recalled some years later, "but our meeting was very brief and I was not really aware he had taken much notice of me. So I was surprised and pleased when he asked me to appear with him in Madrid. I was actually filming there at the time so it all worked out very well."

Bob particularly wanted to film a musical number with Gina

to be used in his TV show for screening in America, and unbeknownst to her had cabled the agents of NBC TV in Spain to find out whether her singing in any way matched her stunning, buxom beauty. The reply he got still brings a smile to his face when he recalls it.

"I sent this cable, 'Find out if Lollobrigida can sing'" he says, "and then I waited for the reply. It came the next day. The message said, 'She sins as well as she acts'. The missing letter made it read better than any joke of mine! But I needn't have worried because it turned out her notes were as well rounded as the rest of her."

Gina herself takes up the story. "I was a bit nervous about singing on the show, but Bob said I could do one of my favourite songs *and* I could sing in Italian. So I decided on, "Non Dimenticar" (Don't Forget). The audience were wonderful."

Bob has described her impact on the several thousand servicemen crowded into a huge aircraft hangar on the Torrejon air base near Madrid in a typically more fulsome manner. "Looking at her sultry loveliness, I realised why pizza had become Italy's second dish. I have to say that although probably not too many of the boys in the audience understood Italian, as Gina stood in the spotlight shimmering in a gold lamé sheath dress they got her message all the same!"

Gina had also been worried about how she would appear on TV when filmed in an aircraft hangar — but again the camera did her more than justice.

"Later in my career when I went to Hollywood I very nearly worked on a movie with Bob," Gina said recently in Rome where she has now turned her back on films to become a leading executive with a cosmetic firm. "I am not surprised that he has remained so popular all these years because of his sheer energy and enthusiasm."

Gina also happens to be an outstanding photographer and among her vast collection of pictures is, not surprisingly, one of the unmistakable features of Bob Hope!

Jill St.John

This stunning redhead was Bob's co-star on his — quite literally — "explosive" first visit to Vietnam at Christmas 1964. A former child star on the radio at the tender age of 6, Jill had made her mark in films as an empty-headed, well-built broad, but is, in fact, highly intelligent with a most engaging personality. She remembers what was to prove the first of several of Bob's visits to Vietnam with understandable clarity:

"I'm full of admiration for Bob, for nothing fazes him when he has to perform — neither fatigue nor fear. I remember when we were in Vietnam during the worst of the fighting — the winter of 1964–5. We had done a show for the GIs at Bien Hoa, and then we were supposed to fly into Saigon. We got held up about 20 minutes because of some mishap involving Barney McNulty, who had been Bob's cue-card

Opposite:
Gina Lollobrigida: "Looking at her sultry loveliness, I realised why pizza had become Italy's second dish."

man for years. During the delay, the Vietcong blew up the Brinks Hotel across the street from the Caravelle Hotel where we were supposed to stay in Saigon. Everyone else was spooked out by this — but it didn't bother Bob in the least. He just went to his room which was strewn with shattered glass and fell asleep until it was time to go and do the show. He has the rare ability to sleep or take cat-naps anywhere!"

Interestingly, Barney McNulty, a veteran member of Bob's crew, has filled in the remaining details of Jill's story:

"What happened was that I had about 300 heavy cue-cards propped up on a stand at Bien Hoa and the stand collapsed under the weight just as we were finishing the show. It took me 20 minutes to pick up the cue-cards and get them back in order again. That set back our schedule and was the time when the Cong bombed the Brinks Hotel.

When I later met General Westmoreland who was in

Jill St. John: "When she walked out on stage she looked as if she had stepped out of the beauty salon at Vidal Sassoon."

charge of the American forces, he told me he had heard evidence that a Cong murder squad had been riding around with a bomb in a pick-up truck waiting for us to arrive. The General said their written orders were to kill Bob and the rest of us to embarrass the South Vietnam government over not being able to protect such important visitors. When we didn't show up on schedule, the Cong assassination team hit the next best available target, the Brinks, which was a kind of officer's billet.

Do you know what Bob said about all this? He said, 'Saved by the idiot cards again!'"

Jill was reunited again with Bob for a Christmas Show in 1971, and though it was in a much more peaceful locality, Spain, the schedule proved just as hectic to fulfil:

"Because of my commitments, it wasn't possible for me to catch up with Bob on the tour until he was due in Vicenza in northern Italy. Well, in Los Angeles I found I couldn't get a direct flight to Rome, so I flew to New York and then after a three hour wait, jetted on to London. In London there was no direct flight to Vicenza, so I had to take a plane to Rome. By the skin of my teeth I caught the last train out of Rome to Vicenza — only to find when I got there, Bob and his party were already on their way to Madrid!

I got this message from Bob begging me to follow him to Spain. I'd already been on the move for 24 hours so I thought, 'What the hell!' Finally, I grabbed an Iberian flight out of Rome to Madrid and landed in Spain after 56 hours travelling. How I did that show I'll never know. The things Bob Hope can get people to do!"

Bob has paid his own tribute to this remarkable round-the-world dash to join the show: "I just don't know what it is that Jill has. She either has great bounce or a masterful will — but when she walked on that stage she looked as if she'd just stepped out of the beauty salon at Vidal Sassoon. And *what* a reception she got!"

Jill is also remembered for a memorable on-stage exchange with Bob — which, despite getting the nationality of one of the individuals wrong (Sean Connery is actually a Scotsman!), is still very funny.

"You've played passionate love scenes with Frank Sinatra, with Sean Connery and with me," he said. "How do we compare?"

"Well, Bob," she replied. "Frank is a typical Italian. He's passionate, fiery, always the lover. And Sean Connery, well he's a typical Welshman. He's savage, untamed, primitive, forceful. You know — he's all man. And you — you're a typical Californian."

"Wait a minute," said a puzzled Bob, "A typical Californian?"

"Yes," nodded the lovely redhead, "nothing will move you but an earthquake!"

Carroll Baker

Carroll, who was Bob's co-star on his 1965 trip to Thailand and Vietnam, had become famous for her role as the seductive nymphet in *Baby Doll* (1956) and was then being groomed as Marilyn Monroe's successor in pictures such as Harold Robbins' *The Carpetbaggers* (1964), and *Harlow*, which she completed just before making the Christmas tour. Unknown to Bob, however, Carroll was in the middle of a dispute with Paramount Pictures when she left for Vietnam, a fact which she did not reveal until later. "I was so grateful for the chance to go with Bob to entertain the troops that Christmas. It was a chance to get out of myself and do something special for someone else and also leave my problems behind."

Carroll's impact on the troops was indeed "special" as Bob himself has recalled:

"She was one of the most succulent dishes I'd ever put on the menu for those lonely G.I.s. The only problem was that whenever she'd been promoting her films, the clothes she had worn had been so revealing that she'd become known as 'The Transparent Blonde'. It took us quite some time to find a few gowns that I figured wouldn't heat up the war too much and could be shown on TV without getting us an X-rating!"

Carroll herself naturally prefers to remember the shows rather than her wardrobe.

"Although I'd appeared mostly in films, my early career had been on the stage and I was so happy to have the chance to appear live before a live audience once again. Especially working with someone like Bob who has such a rapport with big crowds.

Those ten days in Vietnam were very tough going, though, even dangerous at times, but they were a real tonic for me. After the shows we went to the hospitals and when I held the hands of some of those damaged young men I realised that my pain was not exclusive. That there were others suffering much more terrible things than I was.

Actually, when we got back to Los Angeles after those gruelling days in Southeast Asia, everyone said the same thing. 'It's unbelievable — we all look and feel like Death warmed over. But Carroll looks better now than when she left!' I'm pretty sure that no one was aware of the deep depression I'd been in before going to Vietnam.

It was a very special trip for me, and I'll always treasure the memory of the comedy routines I did with Bob and the happy smiles on the faces of those boys who could forget that terrible war at least for a few hours."

Raquel Welch

Described as "the undisputed sex goddess of the sixties", Raquel got tremendous personal satisfaction as well as an overwhelming reception when she was Bob's co-star on his

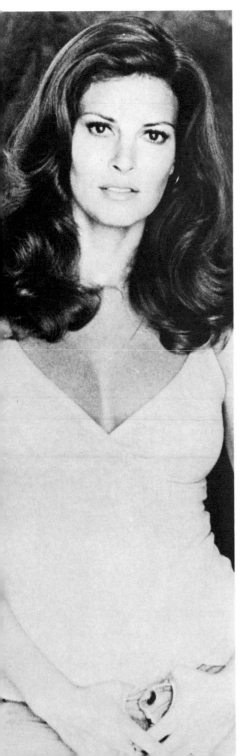

Raquel Welch: "Even standing still she could outperform most so-called sex bombs at their shimmiest."

1967 Christmas revisit to Vietnam. Raquel, the Californian beauty queen whose sheer determination and energy — not to mention her voluptuous figure and sensuous face — had first won her film contracts and then made her one of the highest paid stars in the entertainment business, was just winning international attention when Bob spotted her.

"The year before that I had made a couple of movies, *One Million Years BC* and *Fantastic Voyage*," Raquel says, "but I guess I was best known for all that publicity rather than my acting ability. In fact, to be quite honest, before making the trip to Vietnam I thought being me was a bum rap. Then the first day there they had these great big posters of me everywhere and the reception the boys gave me was absolutely wonderful!"

Bob had been determined to take someone really stunning with him to Vietnam that Christmas after receiving a touching letter from a G.I. serving in the country appealing for some beauty to brighten up "this muddy hell". The comedian later explained how he came to pick Raquel:

"Like a weather watcher, I take a certain pride in being able to detect hurricanes before they happen, and that year I really found one: Hurricane Raquel. Up to that time Raquel Welch had appeared mainly on European magazine covers. She had played in some movies, but she was best known for an appearance in which she never spoke a line, or even moved — a publicity poster for *One Million Years BC* in which she just stood there in a furry Stone Age bikini. Even standing still, Raquel could outperform most so-called sex bombs at their shimmiest!"

Raquel, however, had no intention of standing still on the show, and wearing a tiny blue-and-white knitted mini-skirt, she danced and sang for the troops — even inviting a lucky handful of them to join her on stage and dance. Bob commented afterwards, "I've never seen anything like it — I'm sure that even guys with their legs in plaster would have thrown away their crutches to join her doing the Watusi!"

Neither was Raquel content with just appearing on stage. "During our stay in Vietnam, Bob and I visited some of the field hospitals to meet the guys who had been wounded," she recalls. "Some of them had terrible injuries, but they never complained. It was all I could do to fight back the tears and smile at them."

Bob was just as full of praise for his co-star. "She was like all the great pros — they adapt to any situation and work under any conditions. Raquel could drive you crazy about make-up and how much bosom she could show without getting arrested, and so on, but when it came to putting on the show all the flaky stuff ended. She got it all together — that chick knew how to please an audience!"

After a gruelling tour which included 21 shows and visits to six hospitals in the combat zones, it was an exhausted but exhilarated Raquel who flew back to America.

"Everywhere we went I could see just how much the tour meant to those boys and it was all just so worthwhile," Raquel told journalists on her arrival. A little later she was featured extensively in the Bob Hope TV Special made about the trip and screened on NBC.

International fame was now just around the corner for her — and Raquel and Bob were actually reunited again when this had been fully established. It occurred in London in 1979 when she appeared in a televised show from the London Palladium, starring Bob, and performed a song and dance routine hailed in the British press as "a knock out". Bob's comment was even more succinct, "I tell you, she's *all* woman!"

Ann-Margaret

Ann-Margaret, the Swedish-born actress, singer and dancer who accompanied Bob on the 1968 tour of the East — taking

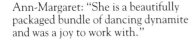

Ann-Margaret: "She is a beautifully packaged bundle of dancing dynamite and was a joy to work with."

in Japan, Korea, Taiwan, Thailand, Vietnam, Okinawa, the Philippines and Guam — earned this credit from Bob on her return, "She was my number one It girl!" Ann-Margaret became famous for her lively performance in *Bye-Bye Birdie* in 1963, and was thereafter cast in a number of song and dance pictures aimed at younger audiences, in particular a co-starring role with Elvis Presley in one of his best movies, *Viva Las Vegas*, made in 1964. Later, Ann-Margaret diversified her undoubted talent by playing in several dramatic movies as well as cabaret in some of the top Las Vegas nightspots. In fact, the success of her tour with Bob in 1968 was instrumental in this major change in her career.

"Actually, the tour with Bob was very nearly a non-starter for while we were rehearsing the show in Tokyo a number of performers — including me — went down with a kind of Asian flu," Ann-Margaret recalled later. "By the end of that rehearsal I could hardly speak above a whisper, let alone sing. But Bob said we had to go on — and go on we did!"

Even though she was initially singing below her best, Ann-Margaret was a hit from the very first show. The mini-skirt she wore, plus knee-high boots and a sable coat, helped a great deal — as did what Bob later described as "her kittenish sexiness that turned on the boys much more than any blatant bump and grind could have!"

She herself has always seen her act in a very personal way. "I don't think I'm a singer and dancer who also acts, or an actress who sings and dances. I'm an entertainer, *that's* what!"

During their Christmas together, Ann-Margaret became very impressed by Bob's mastery of an audience and now puts him on a par with another of America's greatest comedians — who also happens to be a friend of Bob's — George Burns.

"Actually, we mentioned George during a bit of the show we did together," she recalled. "Bob said to me at one stage, 'I hear that you were discovered by George Burns at the Sahara Hotel in Las Vegas.' I replied, 'Yes, and I think he is the world's funniest comedian.' At which he glared at me for a bit and then said, 'Well, he's all right — but he's no Spiro Agnew!'" (Agnew was then Vice-President of the US and noted for his dour nature.)

After the problems of the flu epidemic, the party might well have hoped that all their bad luck was behind them. But not so. Ann-Margaret remembers:

"While we were flying from Bangkok to Vietnam, someone noticed that one of the engines had begun to smoke. But before anyone had a chance to get nervous, Bob started cracking jokes, and while we were laughing the crew stopped the engine and extinguished the fire. Bob's a great man to have around in an emergency!"

Ann-Margaret and Bob visited a number of the front-line hospitals to cheer up wounded soldiers, an experience which deeply moved the young singer. "One of the songs I most like

Opposite:
Ursula Andress: "All she had to do was stand there — the vibrations took care of the rest."

102

doing on stage is 'When You're Smiling', and when one of the men in the hospital asked me to sing it, it brought tears to my eyes. But I gave it to them twice and it was really wonderful to hear everyone joining in."

On his return to America, Bob's verdict on his 1968 co-star was short and emphatic, "Ann-Margaret is a beautifully packaged bundle of dancing dynamite — a joy to work with."

Ursula Andress

This voluptuous Swiss-born actress, described at the high-point of her career as "The Most Beautiful Girl in the World", accompanied Bob on his 1970 Christmas tour which virtually spanned the world. Beginning in England, the party entertained American troops in Germany, Crete, Bangkok, Thailand, Vietnam, Korea and Alaska. It was a demanding but nonetheless rewarding experience for Ursula who was well known to all the servicemen for her stunning appearance in the first James Bond film, *Dr. No* (1962). She recalls their first meeting:

"I really had no idea what the tour would involve. In fact, I remember saying to Bob Hope, 'I can't sing and I can't dance so what do you want me to do?' He just smiled and said, 'Just stand there — the audience will do the singing and the dancing!'

It was a good joke and it helped put me at my ease, because you see I am not good at taking on obligations and responsibilities. In fact, I hate to have them. But then I also know that if you run away from everything, you become nothing. You might just as well stay in one dark room and dream your time away.

But those American boys were so enthusiastic, so appreciative, that I enjoyed all the little comedy routines I did with Bob and they seemed to like me, too."

Undoubtedly one of the things the troops liked was the eye-popping outfit that Ursula wore: velvet shorts and tights and a body-hugging long-sleeved top. Bob recalls,

"I lost a lot of the boys' attentions the minute that Ursula Andress walked on. When she slinked onstage in those lavender tights she caused more flashbulbs to pop than anyone else in the show. The troops were running down the aisles, waving their cameras, shouting, whistling, and I was right — all she had to do was stand there. The vibrations took care of the rest."

Ursula wore that fantastic costume even when the party went from the steaming heat of Bangkok to the freezing cold of Alaska — and as a result was feted by the servicemen both on stage and off.

"Bob made me feel comfortable on stage because he was already something of an institution with the American forces and I know that most of them really respected him for giving up his Christmas every year to entertain them.

Dolores Hope (who appeared with her husband on his final overseas Christmas show in 1972): "Underneath that smooth, unruffled exterior is one of the hardest working guys you'll ever meet."

He really loves his audiences, and because love has always been the most important thing in my life I was glad to have been on the tour. Of course, it proved to be one of his last, which also made it a bit special."

Dolores Hope

In fact, Bob made another tour in 1971, in which he was reunited with Jill St. John, and then a year later undertook what proved to be, "The Last Christmas Show". Again he visited Vietnam, but this time his co-star was none other than his wife, Dolores, formerly, of course, a singing star herself. It seemed a fitting climax to a quarter of a century of entertaining troops to be accompanied by the person who had so steadfastly supported him through all the years and seemingly been happy to be parted from him at that most festive time of the year.

Dolores commented after the tour, "Bob seems to have been off entertaining the troops ever since we were married. People keep asking me whether I resented all the time he was away, but knowing how much good he was doing helping to keep our boys entertained, how could I object?"

Did she mind him spending all that time with some of the world's most famous sex symbols?

"No. You see, though he's remarkable in many ways —
especially the love he seems to draw from his audiences —
he's basically an ordinary, decent human being. I've been
asked what is the recipe for Bob's longevity and I answer in
two words: hard work. Don't ever be fooled by his relaxed,
easy-going manner. Underneath that smooth, unruffled
exterior is one of the hardest working guys you've ever met.
It's been that way ever since I've known him, and it'll be
that way until the day he dies."

12
The
Band of
Hope

"The King of One Liners", a cartoon of Bob drawn by one of his comedy writers in 1980.

For a comedian who has been in the eye of the media for so long, it comes as no surprise to learn that some remarkable "titles" have been credited to Bob Hope during his 60-year career in show business.

"The longest-running one-line stand-up snap-it-out comedian in the history of show business," the American magazine *Time* described him as long ago as October 1963. "The master mechanic of comedy" was the British *Daily Mail's* label in December 1977. *Rolling Stone* went even further in March 1980 calling him "The most famous and well-travelled funnyman alive". While most recently of all, the prestigious *New York Times* referred to him in April 1986 as quite simply "The King of One-Liners".

If there is a suggestion of flippancy in some of these titles — and Bob himself is more than a little prone to flippancy — there is certainly nothing flippant about his attitude to what has been his life's work: comedy. His views on his art are strongly held and discussed with the assurance of hard-won experience.

"The whole basis to doing comedy is timing," he says, his face set with a seriousness rarely observed when he is performing. "The thing of letting an audience discover a joke is the greatest form of entertainment. Take an example. I can say, 'I went to the ticket desk at Kennedy Airport and said I'll take two chances to London.' The audience don't at first see it's a joke and then they start to nudge each other.

"There is also a lot of technique involved about working with comedy," he continues. "Such as running away from a punch line — that is to speak the joke quickly without pausing for the punch line. It's like a magician trying to hide the trick."

Like a magician, too, Bob knows that his delivery is vitally important, and indeed whenever he talks about his craft he will often jump up and use his arms to give more emphasis to what he is saying. But there is no mystery, he claims, about how he creates his jokes.

"What is needed in comedy isn't just the jokes or the timing or standing still and looking at an audience. It is being topical and knowing what to cut out. What I do is edit the material my writers provide. I give them a list of topics before every show, then they write a series of gags or jokes on each topic.

Then these are all typed up on what we call the points sheet and I tick off the ones I'll use and we work out the best running order. I discard at least half of them, sometimes more. That is the key. I try to appear 'pseudosmart'. Not too smart to be way over the heads of the audience — but just the occasional quick sophisticated gag which doesn't matter if they don't get it.

I enjoy putting a show together. The whole thing is knowing what people will laugh at and being accurate most of the time. It comes from experience. People laugh at the

Bob on the receiving end of a practical joke from director George Marshall and some of his co-stars during filming of *Monsieur Beaucaire* in 1946.

same things now that they always have. Audiences still find laughs in parodies of current events and jokes about politicians, booze, drugs, fads, the President, celebrities and sports.

I try and deliver a joke without offending anyone, though I'm never quite sure how it works. I know a lot of the people personally and I know when something will hurt them. I can get away with nuances and insinuations that will only sting them a little."

Being topical and having a constant flow of new material is the reason why Bob has for many years had a full-time staff of writers — never less than four, and in his busiest years sometimes twice that number — who can cost him a whacking £500,000 a year in salaries but provide an endless flow of material. ("Thus each Hope joke is worth roughly the cost of a natural pearl!" *Time* magazine once wryly commented.)

The comedian himself has referred to this team as "The Band of Hope", though the men have nick-named themselves "The NAFT Squad" after Bob's frequent emergency telephone calls which can come at any time and from anywhere around the world and are always preceded by the words, "Need A Few Things, fellas!"

The demands on these men and their capacity to provide new jokes can be judged from just a few simple statistics. In 1952, for instance, the London *Sunday Dispatch* estimated that Bob was then cracking about 100 jokes in every performance he gave and needed about 2,000 "new or renovated gags" every year! Moving on to 1983, *Time* magazine reported that Hope's "rapid-fire rhythm has been clocked at 44 jokes in four minutes" — though by 1977 this had slowed to "the rate of six every minute" according to the *Daily Mail*: facts which must have been something of a relief to the NAFT Squad!

Bob has never made any bones about the importance of these men in his work. In fact, a show business legend has it that he once waved a script at his writers and said, "This is all the talent I have, fellows!" What *is* undisputed is that even if a joke falls flat he never takes it out on his writers.

"When I started I used to sit up all night with a guy called Willy Mahoney writing a radio show called 'Hollywood Parade'. We did it with Dick Powell, that was in 1937–8. It was too much hard work. Now my writers write everything for me — they work on my shows, TV, benefits, etc. With my schedule, I've just got to have good gag men!"

Heading this Band of Hope is executive writer-producer Mort Lochman who has been with Bob ever since he left university over thirty years ago. Fiercely loyal to his boss, Mort has a wealth of funny stories about the demands Hope puts on the team, but is reluctant to discuss the man himself.

"I remember he called us from London once when he was appearing in the Royal Variety Show. He said to me, 'How about a few gags about me and four other guys sharing a dressing room?' Within an hour we phoned back with five quickies — one of which he used: 'The committee gave me a dressing room with four guys and Tanya the Elephant. After 15 minutes the elephant got up and opened the window!'

On another occasion he was on a tour of military bases and suddenly noticed the plane we were flying in was going to land on grass. 'Quick,' he said, 'give me a couple of grass-runway jokes.' Can you imagine! But we came up with one and when Bob landed he quipped, 'I want to thank the fellas who mowed the runway.'"

Two former members of the team who have talked about their boss are an American, Charlie Lee, and the top British comic, Bob Monkhouse, a former freelance writer before becoming a comedy star in his own right. Says Charlie Lee, "Bob likes his humour to be sharp and up to the minute. He wants comment on a person or a situation in the news. Although this might sound pretentious, the form of a Bob Hope script is as stylised as a speech by the President!

Another gag up his sock? Bob was a fast-talking, quick-acting English butler in one of his best pictures, *Fancy Pants*, made in 1950.

Bob is a wonderful audience for a joke and a naturally funny man. He can supply as many cracks as his writers can dig up for him, if not more, and he is full of suggestions for making good jokes better. Mind you, he expects his writers always to be on hand. I remember he once telephoned a guy who was actually on his honeymoon. 'I trust,' he said, 'that I'm not interrupting anything?'"

Bob Monkhouse, now one of the most familiar faces on British television, remembers Hope with great admiration, but can also testify, from personal experience, to the demands he puts on his gag men.

"He was a hard taskmaster who expected his writers to devote every moment of their time to the serious business of making him funny," says Monkhouse who worked for Bob in the fifties with his partner Denis Goodwin.

"He has one foot in the music hall and the other in the electronic age," Bob goes on, attempting to define the style of the man he believes to be the finest stand-up comedian of modern times.

"The combination is unbeatable. he can get away with gags which simply would not be funny with anyone else. When Denis and I presented him with our first script he went through the 120 different gags we had written and picked out a dozen — just like that. I was immediately impressed with his professionalism. Once we were on his payrole we found him even more exacting. If you took a nap he woke you up to ask if you were thinking. I remember we were working in the Dorchester once and Denis went to the toilet. Hope came in and asked where he was, so I told him. Hope then rapped on the door and shouted, 'You got paper in there? Write!'"

Bob Monkhouse believes that the jokes of this master among comics have a unique quality about them. He explains, "Only Hope could get away with, 'Certainly I am English. I'm so English that if you cut me, I bleed tea!'"

It is obvious from such stories that the NAFT Squad produce a vast amount of material that is never used. And though it has been claimed that what Bob Hope leaves *out* of his act would make the career of a lesser comic, nothing is ever wasted or thrown away. All the discarded jokes are filed away under subject matter and cross-referenced to where — if anywhere — they were used, and stored in a vast underground vault at Bob's home which is now so big it requires a full-time archivist. At the last count, there were an estimated seven million jokes on file!

Though Bob prides himself on being able to remember large numbers of jokes, he can also ad-lib brilliantly when the occasión demands. Mental training is the key, he says.

"I've been in the comedy business so long that I've got a comedian's mind — a sort of special mechanism that enables me to build up jokes and then knock them down. For example, I might say, 'I've just come back from Monte Carlo — it's a wonderful place. The sight of those beautiful mountains — and the losers jumping off them. Everybody in Monte Carlo is terribly rich. The other day the police picked up a man with 50,000 francs in his pocket. They arrested him for vagrancy!' See the idea? You just get a subject and push it around."

For a man who has been "pushing around" comedy for half of this century, Bob still says of his art, "There's no great

Some meatball! Bob played a
Broadway critic in the film *Critic's
Choice* (1963).

secret. Keep the excitement going. It makes your adrena-
lin pump, and keep moving all the time. Never stop or they've got
you! Actually, a lot of people don't know they have comic
ability. If they could get a good script they could become good
comedians."

Bob sums up his enduring popularity as a master of mirth
with a touch of philosophy:

"Comedy is a business, you know, and you have to work at
it to be successful. People think a comedian just goes out
on stage and tells jokes. But there's much more to it than
that. I do every show like it's my last one, my last chance.

I want to be remembered only for the laughter. If people
just smile a little when they think of me and remember that
we've had a little fun — that'll be enough. Mind you, I
don't intend to leave — dying can ruin your whole career!
But if I have to go I'd like my tombstone to read, 'As I was
saying . . .'"

13
Pseudo smarts

"My Age? If you deduct the amount of time I've spent at airports searching for my luggage I'm only 43!"

"Pseudosmarts — that's the way I describe my stuff. I want the audience to enjoy it like I do." A quote by Bob Hope in Time magazine, May 1983. Here are a selection of some of his best one-liners.

"I don't know what other career I could have had — I thought of politics, but I'm not that good an actor."

———

"I didn't get to go to college until I played a Harvard man in Son of Paleface."

———

"I have four or five writers — but I write most of the smart gags myself."

———

"I have this terrific make-up man — but he's expensive: I have to bring him in from Lourdes."

———

"Last year I took this vacation cruise in Canada but I got bored — fish don't applaud."

———

"I'm learning humility — I called my agent today and asked if there was any more room on Mount Rushmore."

———

"You know if I had the kind of money they say I have I wouldn't have gone to Vietnam — I'd have sent for it."

———

"My oil wells? — I get as much as George Raft gets out of his comb at the end of the week."

———

"A guy I know was asked if he was a Jehovah's witness — 'Hell, no', he said, 'I didn't even see the incident.'"

———

"Some friends of mine had a very exclusive wedding — they threw a Chinaman with every grain of rice."

———

"How about the Teamsters Union guys who picketed the reindeer last Christmas for carrying freight without a Teamsters card?"

———

"I loved the April Fools' gag a fellow pulled in Washington — he walked into the White House and said he was from Missouri and before he could holler, 'April Fool', he was a Cabinet member."

The price of one joke too many? A juxtaposition of film stills that would surely delight the joker in Bob! (Above) Facing the chop in *Casanova's Big Night* (1954) and up to his neck in trouble in *Call Me Bwana* made in 1963.

"I really wish one of the Presidential Candidates would pick Charlton Heston as his running mate — we sure could do with a miracle."

―――――

"I want to tell you that Ronald Reagan is a great showman — he could sell a Datsun to Lee Iacocca."

―――――

"My age? If you deduct the amount of time I've spent at airports searching for my luggage I'm only 43."

―――――

"You know, I once stepped off a plane into so much mud that my alligator shoes thought they were coming back to life."

―――――

"Did you read about Howard Hughes disappearing? — the next day Jack Benny showed up at the police station and claimed to be his only son."

―――――

"I sensed I was getting older last week when a Boy Scout helped me across the street — and it was George Burns."

―――――

"You know, George Burns says when he wakes up he checks the papers — and if he's not in the Obituary Column he orders breakfast."

―――――

"Actually I still feel very young: I got up this morning and finished 50 push-ups — mind you I started them in 1974."

―――――

"I have to keep working because I can only play one game of golf a day."

―――――

"I wanna tell you that baseball is the only game you spend eight months of the year on grass and not get busted."

―――――

"You show me a man who doesn't watch football on Sunday and I'll show you a man whose wife could play tackle for any team."

―――――

"Do you know they never touch beer in Germany? — even my bath had a head on it."

―――――

"Everywhere I looked in Greece there were ruins. I saw a Sergeant with one last night."

"Long dresses on women don't bother me — I've got a good memory."

———

"I see some women are wearing leather pantsuits — when they bend over they look like lumpy billfolds."

———

"Do you know I travel so much the towels in my bathroom say 'Hers' and 'Welcome Stranger'."

———

"Want to know what a smartass is? — a kid who can sit on an ice cream cone and tell you the flavour."

———

"I wanna tell you I could have retired years ago but I have a government to support."

———

"Travelling Hope-fully" 10: The two entertainers greet their wives at the end of the world tour in 1944.

"I'd carry a camel a mile to hear ten people laugh."

14
The Great Swinger

"My golf handicap? It needs repair. If I was a prizefighter, they'd stop it!"

Bob Hope talking in 1983

Although Bob has always been quick to make fun of his prowess as a golfer, the game remains one of the passions of his life and he has always played with great seriousness. Indeed, when he was playing at his very best in the 1950s his handicap was a remarkable 4, and even recently he was still able to go round an 18-hole course and finish with a score in the high eighties. What has never varied, though, is his almost classic golf swing.

Curiously, for one with such a fascination with the game, it is interesting to learn that he didn't first become involved with it by working as a caddy.

"Caddying was one of the few things I didn't do as a boy in Cleveland. In my early twenties I first tried to play golf, but I just couldn't master it. The trouble was I lacked the patience — I stood in one spot on the Cleveland course and flailed away at the ball with very little success. So I went home and burned my clubs!

I didn't touch the game again until I was established in vaudeville in New York and a couple of fellows I was appearing with persuaded me to have a game at the Westchester Club. They gave me a little coaching and after that I couldn't leave the game alone."

Bob's game really began to improve when he moved to Hollywood in the late thirties to commence his film career. There he joined the Lakeside Golf Club in North Hollywood and soon found himself rubbing shoulders with other stars just as hooked on the game as he was. Interestingly, too, in his first major film, *The Big Broadcast of 1938*, he played a scene on the Lakeside course with the great comedian W.C. Fields, himself a golf enthusiast!

A number of the people he played with — including entertainers, business people, politicians and later some of the greatest golfing professionals — became friends, and today he says that his closest pals also happen to be his "golf buddies". In fact, in reply to a recent question about his closest friendships, Bob said, "God, that's a tough, tough question. I've got several of them, but I hate to mention them. I've known these people for 25 or 30 years, but I don't really have anybody in show business that I would say is that close. I have golfing buddies, you see, and things like that."

Nowadays, Bob generally plays on one or other of the four golf courses in Palm Springs (his favourite being the Eldorado) and of course he has the single-hole chip and putt course in the grounds of his home. This constant practice has undoubtedly paid off for he is proud of the fact that he has achieved no less than five holes in one during the 50-odd years he has been playing! (For the last of these he was awarded a special silver cup by *Sports Illustrated* magazine!)

Bob's association with the game is world famous, of course, and among the tournaments named after him, The Bob Hope Classic, held every January in Palm Springs, attracts the largest number of professional players to any such event.

Bob wears a snappy bowler hat while demonstrating his classic golf swing in London in 1953.

(Other similar events have also been held in Britain and Japan.) Similarly, each year he plays in charity tournaments all over the world raising millions of dollars for good causes. (One estimate claims he belongs to 18 clubs which costs him in excess of £50,000 in annual fees, and has played on over 2,000 courses as far apart as St. Andrews in Scotland and the Tokio Golf Club in Japan!) He has also been elected to the Golf Hall of Fame.

Despite this devotion to the game, Bob enjoys being able to laugh about it: and the stories he tells — and those which are told about him by his partners — are legion. A few of the best

Great friends — but fierce golfing rivals: an intimate photograph of Bob and Bing playing a round in 1964.

I think deserve recounting here.

An early story concerns his first return visit to Britain in 1939, during which he and his wife, Dolores, made a detour to Scotland to play at St. Andrews. "When I got there, someone told me, 'Don't miss the cemetery.' I wasn't quite sure what they meant, but I went along anyhow. I'm glad I did. The tombstones were sensational. One read, 'Here lies Sandy McTavish — in heaven. His handicap was seven.'

Dolores Hope enjoyed this trip as much as her husband for she was already a keen golfer herself and was quite capable of matching him stroke for stroke — her handicap at one point being a tenacious 5. On one famous occasion, when the couple were staying in Vienna, Dolores actually beat Bob — and a widely repeated story says she has refused to play him again until he pays her the $1 bet he still owes her!

In Hollywood, Bob found another golf enthusiast in his screen partner, Bing Crosby, and their matches — and light-hearted abuse of each other — made dozens of stories for journalists over the years. In October 1937, for instance, the pair played each other for the title of "Golf Champion of the Entertainment World" — which Crosby won handsomely by 12 strokes!

Nevertheless, Bing could still say of his friend, "I'd rather have him as a partner than an opponent." After which he would break into a smile and add, "That's because he can be pretty sneaky. He'll get out there on the first tee and try to make a match. The first thing he does is talk his opponents out of their handicaps!"

Bob never gave up trying to beat Bing Crosby while the singer was alive, frequently attempting to put him off his game with little jibes. Once, when both were still living in Holly-wood and were playing in a foursome, Bob was asked by one of the golfers about the one-hole course he had just laid out behind his home which was then in the Toluca Lake district.

"It's got four bunkers filled with sand," he said casually as his co-star prepared to drive off from the first tee, "Crosby came up from the beach one day and shook out his pockets!"

Bob has always made a point of packing his clubs whenever he travels abroad, and the comic singer Jerry Colonna who toured with him for years — especially on the trips to enter-tain American troops during World War II and later in Vietnam — has recalled this in his own inimitable fashion. Writing in 1945, Colonna said:

"I remember when we were in the Pacific visiting this tiny little island called Emirau. Just as we were about to land, Bob exclaimed, 'So that's what happened to the divot I dug last month at Lakeside!'

In fact, Hope played golf on every island we visited where there was a golf course. The G.I.s liked to watch him play. It seems that every time he teed off, they had another fox hole! He is really a very fine golfer. I will never forget the day he shot an eagle. I learned a lot that day. Primarily, that eagle meat is tough to eat!"

On a more serious note, Bob himself always remembers with special pleasure when he played in the British Amateur tournament in 1950. Although he lost in the first round, he went back to America a very happy man, telling his golfing buddies: "The guy I played against was helping me so much you'd almost think he wanted me to win!"

Another story of Hope playing golf in Britain comes from a later visit to Edinburgh. On arriving to play a charity match, he discovered that his caddy was to be an elderly Scotsman. Bob enquired of the old man how much experience he had. The Scotsman explained that he had been at the club for 45 years and knew every roll of the green.

Hope then asked, "How are you at finding balls?"

Bob scoring an "Eagle" under the watchful gaze of Bing Crosby and Jerry Colonna! — a cartoon by Sig Vogt.

"Verra good," came the distinctive reply.

"Then find one," said Hope, "and we'll start."

The comedian Jackie Gleason, acknowledged as one of Bob's coterie of golf friends, also has a story to tell about him playing at a charity match — this time in Florida. Gleason explains that three times Bob played his ball into the water on the ninth hole.

"He kept expecting me to say something," Gleason recalls, "but I just sat there serenely puffing on a cigarette. When he finally got over the water, I just said, 'Nice shot.' It nearly killed him!"

According to Jackie Gleason, Bob hates to concede a putt. Most players will do so if the distance between the ball and the hole is 'within the leather' — that is, the distance measured from the handgrip of a club to its head. "Not Bob," says Jackie with a smile, "he always insists on measuring with whatever club has the longest grip. You know, Bob's only departure from sanity is his insistence that he can beat me!"

Hope, by way of reply, has maintained that his old friend "likes a gamble and putts with a swizzle stick!"

Bob has the unique distinction of having played golf with the last nine Presidents of America and has a typically humorous way of discussing these men and their prowess.

"Playing golf with any President is handy," he once said, "If you hit a ball into the rough and it stops near a tree, the tree becomes a Secret Service man and moves away!"

The first President Bob played with was one of his great heroes, Dwight 'Ike' Eisenhower, and he recalls stories of their rounds together with special delight.

Bob with one of his favourite partners, the former President of the USA Dwight D. Eisenhower, pictured at the Bob Hope Classic in Palm Springs, February 1967.

"Once when I played with Ike in Washington, I asked him, 'What do you want to bet?' and he replied, 'I usually play for a dollar, dollar, dollar,' he said. For those not familiar with golf terms, this means a dollar is bet on the first nine holes, another on the second nine, and the third on all eighteen. After we'd struck the bet, Ike said, 'Funny thing — I've just lent a million and a half dollars to Bolivia and here I am playing for a dollar, dollar, dollar!'"

Bob also has fond memories of playing with John F. Kennedy who had a very long, straight drive which he says was characteristic of the forthright nature of the man himself. Likewise, he found President Gerald Ford a keen competitor, though rather prone to slicing his ball off the fairway. Bob recalls:

"I spent three days playing with Gerry a few years back. When we got to the first tee I told the gang my handicap was 19, but one of the fellers insisted I was a 21, giving me two extra strokes. I shot an 80. But I was brought to earth the next day. I shot 95 — so everybody felt better!"

Bearing in mind that Ronald Reagan rose from being a Hollywood actor to President of the US, it is interesting to learn that in the late sixties, Bob was seriously approached by two senators who wanted him to run for President:

"They'd had a poll done which showed that something like 80 per cent of the population would find me acceptable as President. But I said no. It would have meant too much of an upset to my life. I know Ronnie made the transition very successfully. You know, he's full of surprises for me,

There was an unusual partner for Bob and Arnold Palmer when they played an exhibition match at Wentworth, England, in 1965.

Bob enjoying a joke with one of the top current golfers, Sevvy Ballesteros, on the Epsom course in England in September 1980

that guy. A wonderful President. I used to have him on my radio show, way back in the 1940s. He was a liberal democrat in those days. He's seen sense since then!"

Among the famous professionals that Bob has played with are Sam Snead, Arnold Palmer, Jack Nicklaus, Gary Player and Severiano Ballesteros. His games with Arnold Palmer, in particular, have been spiced with good humour, and Bob once referred to Arnold as "the biggest crowd pleaser since the invention of the portable sanitary facilities!" Arnold, for his part, has had the last laugh on his friend by winning the Bob Hope Classic in Palm Springs no fewer than five times!

For years, Bob claimed that if he ever gave up performing he would like to have been a golf pro. Talking to one journalist in 1972, he said, "When I say I'm enthusiastic about my work, I mean it. If I lost my enthusiasm for putting things together, I'd say, 'Yeah, I think I'm going to take it easy!' Well, I'd probably become a golf pro and beat everyone on the course!"

If Bob cannot play as well or as often as he would like today, he still keeps up with the game in the newspapers and on television. And he has one wish for the future.

"I reckon when I reach the end of the road," he says with a twinkle in those brown eyes, "I have a hunch it will be on a golf course somewhere between the 18th hole and the club-house. I guess that's the way to go. Like Bing with a putter in your hand . . ."

15
The Man They Call "Mr. TV"

Bob Hope has been one of the most familiar faces on American television for almost 40 years — a record of longevity that is virtually without parallel in TV history. He was an early star in the medium and actually appeared on what was billed as the first commercial TV programme from the West Coast in 1947. Though to begin with, he admits he was sceptical that TV would *ever* catch on!

Although Britain had opened the world's first television service in November 1936, the first sponsored programmes in America did not begin in New York until 1941. Experiments with the new medium had, however, been going on since the early thirties, and while Bob was appearing in a Broadway musical called *Ballyhoo* in 1932, he and two other members of the cast were asked to appear in a trial programme on the local CBS TV station, W2XAB.

According to Bob, "The little black and white pictures were so bad no one could see me — which was just as well. I remember that everyone involved agreed that TV was never going to make it. How *wrong* can you be!"

When he appeared for the second time in 1947 things were very little better. While he was working on *The Road to Rio* he was asked by Paramount to act as MC on a special show the studio was putting out to launch their new television station in Los Angeles. The "spectacular" was billed as the first commercial TV programme on the West Coast — a first for Bob, but not one he cares to dwell on.

"The thing was there were not many people in Hollywood then who had a TV set," he recalls, "so the show didn't get too many viewers. Which is just as well because it was a stinkeroo. I still couldn't see that TV was going to make it."

By 1949, however, things were very much different. The technical quality of television broadcasting had been improved enormously and there were now 127 TV stations across the US serving approximately two million homes.

Bob himself was now the top film box office draw in America, and when he became aware of just *how* much better TV was and the inroads it looked likely to make into the movies, he scrapped his previous reservations and faced the television cameras once more.

In just one programme, a guest appearance on Ed Sullivan's show, "Toast of the Town", he revealed that he had the skill to master this medium just as he had done the stage, radio and films. His appearance with Sullivan was long remembered for his famous quip: "Ed was on TV two years before it started!"

His formal TV debut occurred the following year on Easter Sunday, 19 April 1950, fronting the "Star Spangled Revue" sponsored by Frigidaire. Because of his position as the top cinema draw, Bob was reportedly paid a fee four times the amount ever paid to a single TV performer! The star-spangled guest list was a forerunner of what was to become the norm in a Hope show: Douglas Fairbanks Jnr., Beatrice Lillie, Dinah Shore, Les Brown's Band of Renown and 75 of the most stunningly beautiful dancers. Bob commented afterwards:

"To my surprise, I was as nervous as a cat. I'd been in front of cameras and microphones for years, but I was as jumpy as if I were just starting in show business. After seeing me on a TV screen, one critic remarked, 'TV is still a baby, but it doesn't need that much changing.' However, when the other votes came in it was decided to let me stay on. In fact, Frigidaire were so happy about the way the first show worked out that they paid lavishly for the next four shows, too!"

When asked if there was much difference between working for TV or the radio, Bob added, "I honestly think the secret of TV is being relaxed, casual and easy. I used to work very fast on radio because I found out when I was working for the soldiers and service audiences that they wanted it fast. When I first carried this technique into television it wasn't too successful, so I've slowed down and that seems to work."

The second "Star Spangled Revue" on 5 July was also something of a milestone in that it presented the TV debuts of Frank Sinatra and Peggy Lee. Bob's screen partner, Bing Crosby, also made his first TV appearance on a telethon which the comedian hosted in June 1952.

In the following year, 1953, Bob added a further "first" to his list when he starred in the first hour-long commercial colour TV show, "The Colgate Comedy Hour".

Since then, "Mr. TV", as he has been called, has appeared in well over 300 TV specials including innumerable guest appearances on other people's shows. He has hosted series such as "Celebrity Golf" and "The Bob Hope Chrysler Theatre" which has presented both drama and comedy, and in which he also occasionally starred.

Although many of Bob's appearances on TV have followed the same pattern — an opening topical monologue of ten minutes, a series of comedy sketches and guest appearances, and a finale invariably including "Thanks for the Memory" — he has remained enormously popular with millions of viewers. Indeed, *Films on TV* magazine recently describing him as "according to any rating standard, among the best loved performers and one of the most watched on the tube".

In recent years, his most eagerly awaited appearances have been those in the "Bob Hope Birthday Specials" which began in May 1978 to mark his 75th birthday and have continued ever since. According to one report, "these annual Birthday Specials have taken on the aura of the celebration of a national monument".

TV Guide has explained how they came about:

"The Specials began in 1978 when the USO, fearful that it was being forgotten in the post-Vietnam period, approached a producer, Jim Lipton, who had produced newly elected President Jimmy Carter's inauguration concert on TV. Lipton (a strange bedfellow for Hope in that he has a background in cultural activities and is the author of a ballot-orientated novel, *Mirrors*) came up with the idea of a

Opposite:
Mick Brownfield's tribute to Bob in the *Sunday Express* Magazine on his 78th birthday in 1981.

COMEDY KING

'special' combining a tribute to the USO with Hope's 75th birthday. The tradition has continued with every Bob Hope birthday since — a sort of Memorial Day replacement for the wartime Christmas shows when Hope entertained the troops overseas.

The shows are likely to go on — for Hope never talks of stopping. Although he did mutter to Lipton that when they have 15 years of shows complete (in 1993) they could 'do a terrific roundup, The Best of the Bob Hope Birthday Specials'. When that programme goes on the air, Bob Hope will be 90."

Just as the lovely women who accompanied Bob on his overseas tours have been happy to talk about their associations with him, so those who have worked with the ageless TV maestro have offered their fascinating comments about the man and his style.

Elliott Kozak (TV agent)
"There isn't a town he can go to where he isn't known. So in a sense he can never be alone. But he never travels with an entourage, and he often goes by himself: just him, a suitcase and his golf clubs. His last surviving weakness is ice cream and lemon pie, and when I'd travel with him, he'd often slip away after a show to some drugstore or old diner for some.

A rather unusual presentation for Mr. TV! While filming in Beirut in 1983, Bob is draped with a *keffieh*, a traditional Arab headdress, by a US Marine.

No matter what, he always gets a rubdown in the evening and then ten or eleven hours of sleep. And the last thing he does at night, regardless of where he is, is to take a little walk for a few miles. And he does another funny little thing late at night. He'll telephone old friends — Phyllis Diller, for instance, or Jack Benny when he was alive — and he'll just tell a few jokes. He's called me at one a.m. in the morning and said, 'Hey, did you hear the one about . . .' Then he'll tell the one joke, wait for the laugh, say absolutely nothing else, and hang up. *Click*."

Jim Lipton (TV producer)

"Bob in private is the same as he is in public. He needles Presidents and other high-ranking people in his monologues and he has no awe of them in his personal life, either. We were thinking of asking Prince Charles and Princess Diana to his 80th Birthday Show, but he said, 'Just tell Charlie that I know all his jokes!'

Once after a long funeral mass at St. Patrick's Cathedral in New York, he walked around the corner and rang the door bell at Cardinal Terence Cooke's residence. He told the young priest who answered the door, 'I just want to use the Cardinal's bathroom. Terry won't mind!'"

Barney McNulty (cue-card man)

Bob and I bicker all the time, mostly about where the cue-cards should be. But he likes me because he says I'm insolent like he is. On the other hand, I've seen him really get mad.

One time was when his brother Jack — who's now dead — came out to tell him he'd arranged for a great audience that night: 300 sailors! Bob went on stage and didn't get a single laugh. The audience was 300 *Dutch* sailors and they didn't understand a word he was saying!"

Phyllis Diller (TV comedienne)

"It's always being said that Bob is helpless without his cue-cards and his host of writers. Well, that's total nonsense. I did one of his specials when he was having a lot of trouble with his eyes. He had had four operations on his left eye, and now his right eye was bothering him, too. Also, I'd forgotten my glasses. So neither one of us could see Barney McNulty's cue-cards which were written in ten inch high letters.

We were doing a sketch about a Santa Claus elf and his wife, and not being able to see the cue-cards, Bob began to ad-lib. I just followed along. We made up a lot of stuff about what we were going to have for dinner — like Mouse Wellington with a blubber soufflé. Good God, Bob is one of the most brilliant ad-libbers in the business!"

Jack Benny (TV comedian)

"It's not enough to just get laughs when you are appearing before a live audience on TV. The audience has to love you. And Bob is one of those rare performers who gets love as well as laughs from his audiences."

Dick Cavett (TV talk show host)

"Bob Hope has always been my hero and the fact that I have made him laugh is one of my fondest memories. Once on my old ABC show I had the dream-come-true experience of having him on for a full 90-minute show. I actually got paid for looking at him and sitting next to him. If this sounds like slobbering awe, it is, largely, just that.

During the show I mentioned to the audience that we tend to forget he was born in England and, feigning an *unintentional* double entendre, said, 'Do you think of yourself as even partially English? I mean, when you hear 'God Save The Queen' does any part of you rise?' The laugh lifted him out of his chair. He then speculated on what my studio would be used for henceforth. Later, backstage, he took me aside and said, 'That "rise" line is a good one. I'm gonna use that over there!'"

Loni Anderson (singer)

"Bob has shapely ladies on his show to ogle, to hug and so on. He also has talented, funny ladies. After my first year at WKRP in Cincinnati, he brought me onto one of his specials as a 'shapely' lady.

In our very first rehearsal I had memorised my lines, and he hadn't, and I kidded him about having to use cue-cards. First he got mad, then he said, 'Hey, you're a *funny* lady!' He's used me that way in sketches ever since. He was the first to recognise I wasn't just another voluptuous dumb blonde, and he kept using me, and encouraging me to be a comedienne — and he turned my whole career around."

Janis Paige (dancer)

"Bob is human like everyone else — he can get annoyed and upset. You can always tell he's upset, though, when he begins singing between his teeth. Once on a show I just couldn't master a dance step I was supposed to do with him. He's been marvellous to me, but when I hear that singing between the teeth, watch out. 'Just do the step,' he said to me icily — and, by God, I did!"

Sammy Davis Jnr. (comedian)

"Bob began using me in his TV shows when I was still doing night clubs in Los Angeles. I used to ask him to give me a big build up when he introduced me. But a few shows later, he just said, 'Ladies and gentlemen, Sammy Davis Jnr.' When I came out on the stage I muttered under my breath, 'Thanks a *lot!*' He whispered back, 'Sam, you don't need the build up any more!' That was the beginning of my confidence in myself."

Gregory Peck (actor)

"I know Bob, but I don't know *who* he is. He doesn't socialise much. Maybe in his personal life he is basically the same man who appears on TV. In other words, what you see is what you get."

Bob with Lucille Ball, one of his
favourite co-stars in both films and
on television.

Lucille Ball (actress)
"I adore and admire Bob, he is such fun to work with. But I do
remember that in the old days when we did films like *The Facts
of Life* he'd drive me crazy because he never wanted to
rehearse! All I can really add is that you spell Bob Hope
C-L-A-S-S!"

16

A Complete Bob Hope Filmography

Bob Hope made his first screen test in Hollywood for William Perlberg in 1930 but no contract was offered. He next appeared before the film cameras while appearing in New York on Broadway, and although some sources have suggested his first screen performance was in a short comedy movie entitled *Loves At Three*, no trace of this has been found. His earliest pictures were, though, short comedies in which he reprised his stage roles as a song and dance man.

GOING SPANISH (Mentone Pictures, 1934)
Musical comedy about a singing group.
Directed by John O'Shaughnessy. Script by William Watson and Art Jarrett.
Starring: Leah Ray, Bob Hope.

SOUP FOR NUTS (Mentone Pictures, 1934)
Musical farce set in New York.
Directed by Milton Schwartzwald. Script by Joe Bannon.
Starring: Phil Evans, Bob Hope.

PAREE, PAREE (Warner Bros, 1934)
Comedy short based on the play "Fifty Million Frenchmen" by Herbert Fields, E. Ray Goetz and Cole Porter.
Directed by Roy Mack. Script by Cyrus Wood.
Starring: Billie Leonard, Charles Collins, Dorothy Stone, Bob Hope.

WATCH THE BIRDIE (Warner Bros, 1935)
Romance plagued by practical jokes.
Directed by Lloyd French. Script by Dolph Singer and Jack Henley.
Starring: Neil O'Day, Arline Dinitz, Bob Hope, George Watts.

THE OLD GREY MAYOR (Warner Bros, 1935)
Tribulations of an eloping couple.
Directed by Lloyd French. Script by Herman Ruby.
Starring: Ruth Blasco, Bob Hope, Lionel Stander, Sam Wren.

SHOP TALK (Warner Bros, 1936)
Problems of an heir to a department store.
Directed by Lloyd French. Script by Burnet Hershey and Jack Henley.
Starring: Bob Hope, George Watts, Marie Nordstrom, Arline Dinitz.

DOUBLE EXPOSURE (Warner Bros, 1936)
Bob as an incompetent photographer.
Directed by Lloyd French. Script by Burnet Hershey and Jack Henley.
Starring: Bob Hope, Jules Epailley, Johnny Berkes, Loretta Sayers.

CALLING ALL TARS (Warner Bros, 1936)
Bob borrows a sailor's suit to impress the girls.
Directed by Lloyd French. Script by Jack Henley and Burnet Hershey.
Starring: Bob Hope, Johnny Berkes, Oscar Ragland.

THE BIG BROADCAST OF 1938 (Paramount, 1938)
Series of musical sketches with Bob as MC.
Directed by Mitchell Leisen. Script by Walter de Leon, Francis Martin and Ken Englund.
Starring: W.C. Fields, Martha Raye, Dorothy Lamour, Bob Hope.

SWING, TEACHER, SWING (Paramount, 1938)
Musical comedy about college entrance examinations.
Directed by Raoul Walsh. Script by Walter de Leon and Francis Martin.
Starring: George Burns, Gracie Allen, Martha Raye, Betty Grable, Bob Hope.

DON'T HOOK NOW (Paramount, 1938)
Bob plays himself in a golf tournament.
Directed by Herbert Poleise. Script by John Hammond.
Starring: Bob Hope, Bing Crosby.

GIVE ME A SAILOR (Paramount, 1938)
Slapstick comedy about life of a naval officer.
Directed by Elliott Nugent. Script by Doris Anderson and Frank Butler.
Starring: Martha Raye, Bob Hope, Betty Grable, Jack Whiting.

Fifty years ago — the embryo star and Martha Raye in *Never Say Die* (1939).

THANKS FOR THE MEMORY (Paramount, 1938)
Humorous story of a struggling novelist and his marriage.
Directed by George Archainbaud. Script by Lynn Starling from the play "Up Pops The Devil" by Albert Hackett and Frances Goodrich.
Starring: Bob Hope, Shirley Ross, Charles Butterworth, Hedda Hopper.

NEVER SAY DIE (Paramount, 1939)
High-spirited farce about hypochondriac millionaire.
Directed by Elliott Nugent. Script by Don Hartman, Frank Butler and Preston Sturges.
Starring: Bob Hope, Martha Raye, Ernest Cossart, Andy Devine.

SOME LIKE IT HOT (Paramount, 1939)
Bob plays quick-witted show business entrepreneur.
Directed by George Archainbaud. Script by Lewis R. Poster and Wilkie C. Mahoney.
Starring: Bob Hope, Shirley Ross, Una Merkel, Gene Krupa.

THE CAT AND THE CANARY (Paramount, 1939)
Terror on the loose in a haunted house.
Directed by Elliott Nugent. Script by Walter de Leon and Lynn Starling from the play of the same name by John Willard.
Starring: Bob Hope, Paulette Goddard, John Beal, George Zucco.

ROAD TO SINGAPORE (Paramount, 1940)
Two fugitives from marriage: the first of the Road pictures.
Directed by Victor Schertzinger. Script by Frank Butler and Don Hartman.
Starring: Bing Crosby, Bob Hope, Dorothy Lamour, Anthony Quinn, Jerry Colonna.

THE GHOSTBREAKERS (Paramount, 1940)
Ghost hunting in an old mansion.
Directed by George Marshall. Script by Walter de Leon.
Starring: Bob Hope, Paulette Goddard, Richard Carlson, Anthony Quinn.

ROAD TO ZANZIBAR (Paramount, 1941)
The trio find laughs and adventure on an African safari: the second Road movie.
Directed by Victor Schertzinger. Script by Frank Butler and Don Hartman.
Starring: Bing Crosby, Bob Hope, Dorothy Lamour, Una Merkel.

CAUGHT IN THE DRAFT (Paramount, 1941)
Bob as a movie star plunged into Army life.
Directed by David Butler. Script by Harry Tugend.
Starring: Bob Hope, Dorothy Lamour, Eddie Bracken, Lynne Overman.

NOTHING BUT THE TRUTH (Paramount, 1941)
A stockbroker gambles on always telling the truth.
Directed by Elliott Nugent. Script by Don Hartman and Ken Englund.
Starring: Bob Hope, Paulette Goddard, Edward Arnold, Leif Erikson.

LOUISIANA PURCHASE (Paramount, 1941)
Comedy about politics and a land investigation.
Directed by Irving Cummings. Script by Jerome Chodorov and Joseph Fields.
Starring: Bob Hope, Victor Moore, Vera Zorina, Don Drake.

MY FAVOURITE BLONDE (Paramount, 1942)
Love and thrills in the world of vaudeville.
Directed by Sidney Lanfield. Script by Don Hartman and Frank Butler.
Starring: Bob Hope, Madeleine Carroll, Gale Sondergaard, George Zucco.

ROAD TO MOROCCO (Paramount, 1942)
The third Road picture poking fun at desert dramas.
Directed by David Butler. Script by Frank Butler and Don Hartman.
Starring: Bing Crosby, Bob Hope, Dorothy Lamour, Anthony Quinn, Dona Drake.

STAR SPANGLED RHYTHM (Paramount, 1942)
Bob again plays MC in variety show.
Directed by George Marshall. Script by Harry Tugend.
Starring: Bob Hope, Betty Hutton, Bing Crosby, Susan Hayward, Dick Powell, Dorothy Lamour, Paulette Goddard.

THEY GOT ME COVERED (Paramount, 1942)
A farcical mix of music, comedy and spies.
Directed by David Butler. Script by Harry Kurnitz.
Starring: Bob Hope, Dorothy Lamour, Otto Preminger, Lenore Aubert.

LET'S FACE IT (Paramount, 1943)
Bob in another comedy of Army life.
Directed by Sidney Lanfield. Script by Harry Tugend.
Starring: Bob Hope, Betty Hutton, Dona Drake, Dave Willock.

A WELCOME TO BRITAIN (Ministry of Information/Stand Pictures, 1943)
Bob introduces a guide to Britain for American servicemen.
Directed by Anthony Asquith and Burgess Meredith. Script by Cecil D. Armstrong.
Starring: Bob Hope, Burgess Meredith, Felix Aylmer, Beatrice Lillie.

HE WAR LOAN DRIVE (US Department of Treasury, 1944)
Second patriotic movie for Bob helping promote savings in USA.
Directed by Michael Ward. Script by T.S. Edmunds.
Starring: Bob Hope, Ann Malloney.

Bob the brave, chin and chest out - in *The Cat and the Canary* (1939) with Paulette Goddard.

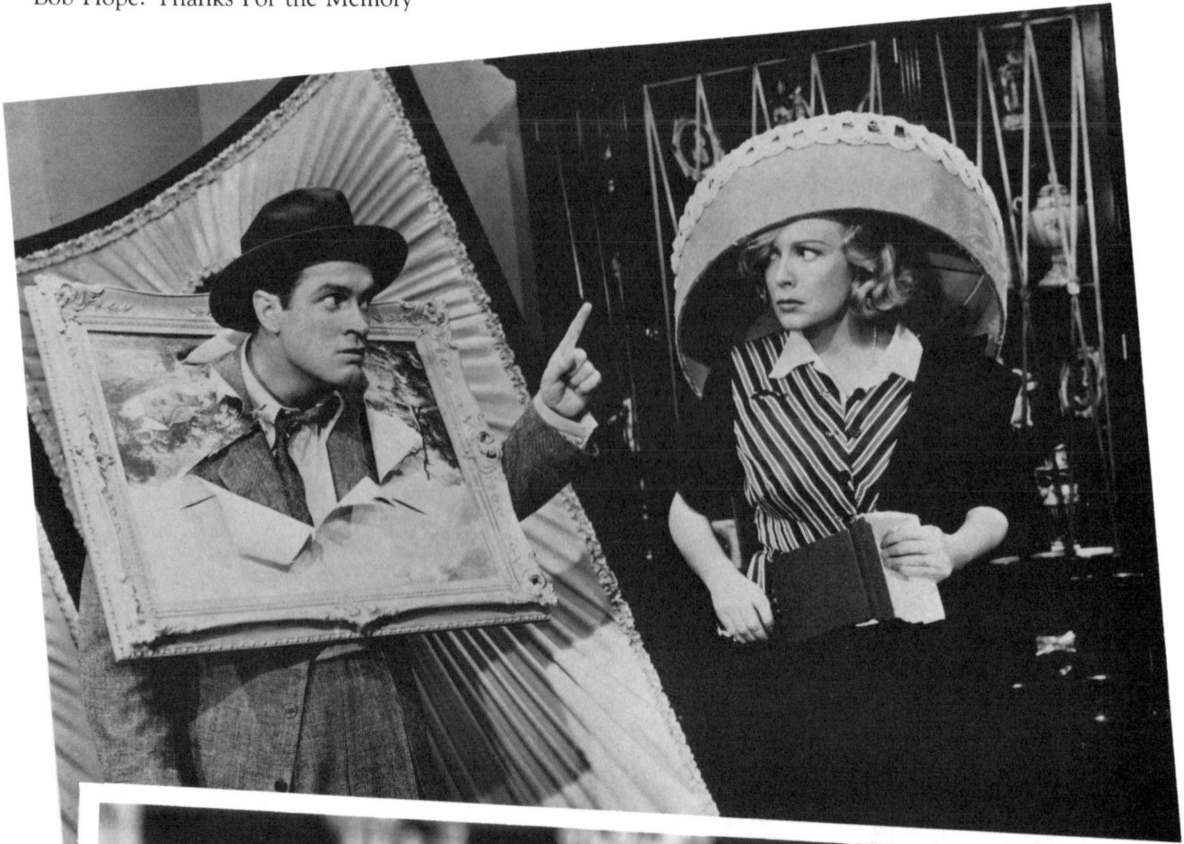

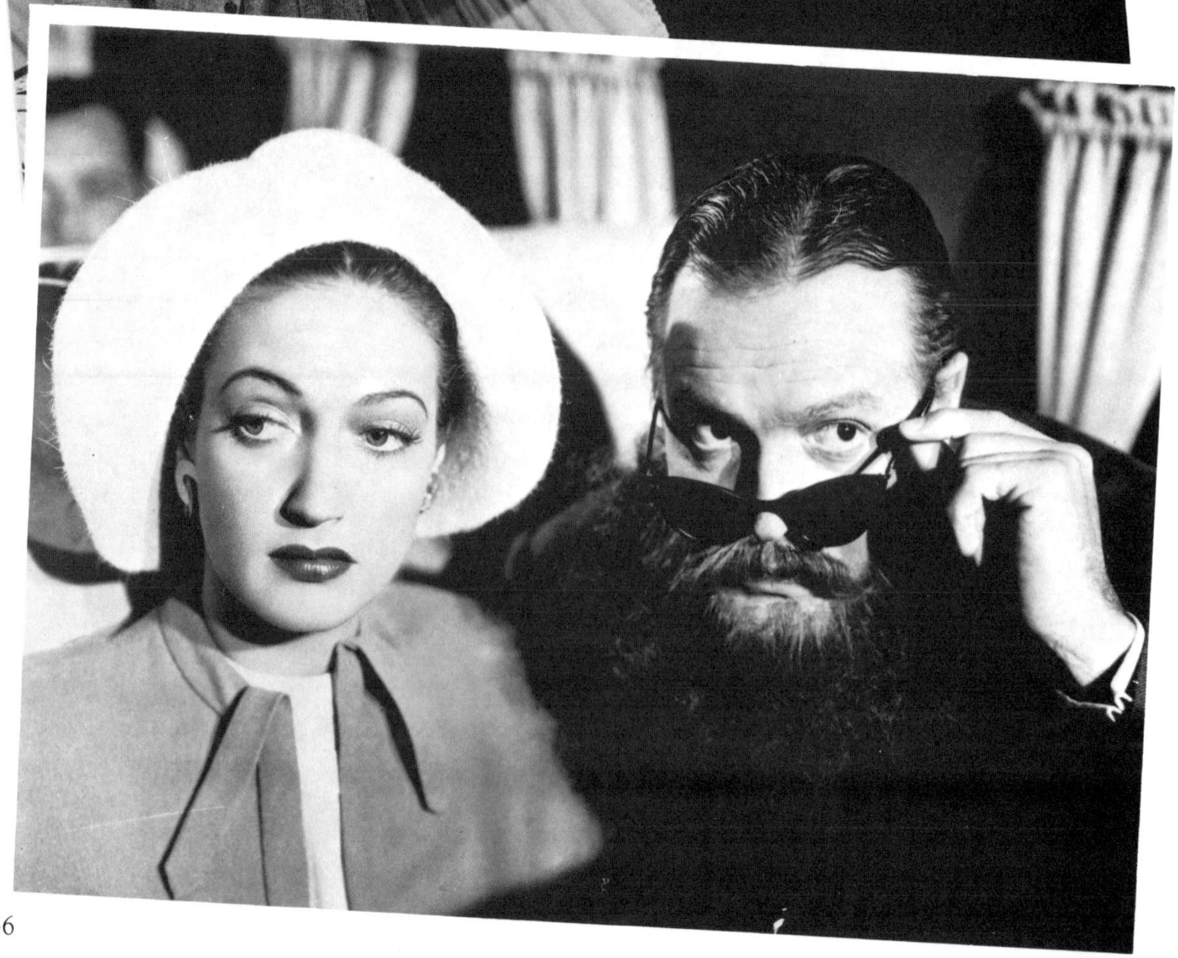

THE PRINCESS AND THE PIRATE
(Samuel Goldwyn/RKO, 1944)
Swashbuckling story of a trick entertainer.
Directed by David Butler. Script by Don Hartman, Melville Shavelson and Everett Freeman.
Starring: Bob Hope, Virginia Mayo, Walter Brennan, Victor McLaglen. With guest appearance by Bing Crosby.

MEMO FOR JOE (New York TB Association, 1944)
A campaigning appearance by Bob to promote the sale of Christmas gift seals.
Directed by Richard Fleischer. Script by Bob Greenman.
Starring: Bob Hope, Tammy Lawson.

ALL STAR BOND RALLY (Fox, 1945)
A variety show promoting the sale of War Bonds for the US Treasury Department.
Directed by Michael Audley. Script by Roland Zammett.
Starring: Bob Hope, Bing Crosby, Frank Sinatra, Betty Grable, Harpo Marx.

HOLLYWOOD VICTORY CARAVAN
(Paramount, 1945)
Celebration of the Allied war efforts.
Directed by William Russell. Script by Melville Shavelson.
Starring: Bob Hope, Bing Crosby, Humphrey Bogart, Betty Hutton, Alan Ladd, Dona Drake.

ROAD TO UTOPIA (Paramount, 1945)
Fourth Road movie set in the cold of Alaska.
Directed by Hal Walker. Script by Norman Panama and Melvin Frank.
Starring: Bing Crosby, Bob Hope, Dorothy Lamour, Hilary Brooke.

MONSIEUR BEAUCAIRE (Paramount, 1946)
Historical comedy about a Spanish barber.
Directed by George Marshall. Script by Melvin Frank and Norman Panama.
Starring: Bob Hope, Joan Caulfield, Patrick Knowles, Marjorie Reynolds.

Two of Bob's most successful films: being 'framed' in *My Favourite Blonde* (1942) with Madeleine Carroll; and heavily bewhiskered with Dorothy Lamour in the "sequel" *My Favourite Brunette* (1947).

MY FAVOURITE BRUNETTE (Paramount, 1947)
Bob the photographer turns amateur detective to solve a mystery.
Directed by Elliott Nugent. Script by Edmund Beloin and Jack Rose.
Starring: Bob Hope, Dorothy Lamour, Peter Lorre, Lon Chaney jnr. Guest appearance by Bing Crosby.

ROAD TO RIO (Paramount, 1947)
Carnival time for the famous trio in the fifth Road film.
Directed by Norman Z. McLeod. Script by Edmund Beloin and Jack Rose.
Starring: Bing Crosby, Bob Hope, Dorothy Lamour, Gale Sondergaard, Jerry Colonna.

VARIETY GIRL (Paramount, 1947)
A star-filled tribute to the Variety Club of America.
Directed by George Marshall. Script by Edmund Hartmann, Frank Tashlin, Robert Welch and Montie Brice.
Starring: Bing Crosby, Bob Hope, Gary Cooper, Ray Milland, Paulette Goddard, Dorothy Lamour, Burt Lancaster.

WHERE THERE'S LIFE (Paramount, 1947)
Farce about a disc jockey who inherits a mythical kingdom.
Directed by Sidney Lanfield. Script by Allen Boretz and Melvin Shavelson
Starring: Bob Hope, William Bendix, George Coulouris, George Zucco.

THE PALEFACE (Paramount, 1948)
Bob as Painless Peter Potter, a dentist married to Calamity Jane.
Directed by Sidney Lanfield. Script by Edmund Hartmann and Frank Tashlin.
Starring: Bob Hope, Jane Russell, Robert Armstrong, Iron Eyes Cody.

SORROWFUL JONES (Paramount, 1949)
Bob in the title role of an inept bookie.
Directed by Sidney Lanfield. Script by Melville Shavelson, Edmund Hartmann and Jack Rose from a play by Damon Runyon.
Starring: Bob Hope, Lucille Ball, William Demarest, Bruce Cabot.

THE GREAT LOVER (Paramount, 1949)
Leader of a boys' group and his exploits on a cruise.
Directed by Alexander Hall. Script by Edmund Beloin, Melville Shavelson and Jack Rose.
Starring: Bob Hope, Rhonda Fleming, Roland Young, Jim Backus.

FANCY PANTS (Paramount, 1950)
Bob as Humphrey an English butler in a comedy drama.
Directed by George Marshall. Script by Edmund Hartmann and Robert O'Brien.
Starring: Bob Hope, Lucille Ball, Bruce Cabot, Jack Kirkwood.

ON STAGE EVERYBODY (Disabled American Veterans Association, 1950)
A warm appeal for the disabled servicemen.
Directed by Jerry Hooper. Script by Jack Rose.
Starring: Bob Hope, Mary West.

THE LEMON DROP KID (Paramount, 1951)
The slapstick story of a racecourse tipster.
Directed by Sidney Lanfield. Script by Frank Tashlin, Edmund Hartmann and Robert O'Brien from a Damon Runyon story.
Starring: Bob Hope, Marilyn Maxwell, Lloyd Nolan, William Frawley.

MY FAVOURITE SPY (Paramount, 1951)
Timid variety artist is mistaken for an international spy.
Directed by Norman Z. McLeod. Script by Edmund Hartmann and Jack Sher.
Starring: Bob Hope, Hedy Lamarr, Francis L. Sullivan, Arnold Moss.

THE GREATEST SHOW ON EARTH (Paramount, 1952)
Bob guests as a member of the circus audience.
Directed by Cecil B. De Mille. Script by Frederic M. Frank, Barre Lyndon and Theodore St. John.
Starring: James Stewart, Betty Hutton, Cornel Wilde, Dorothy Lamour, Bing Crosby.

SON OF PALEFACE (Paramount, 1952)
Spoof western and "sort of" sequel to The Paleface.
Directed by Frank Tashlin. Script by Frank Tashlin, Robert L. Welch and Joseph Quillan.
Starring: Bob Hope, Jane Russell, Roy Rogers, Iron Eyes Cody.

ROAD TO BALI (Paramount, 1952)
Exotic locations for the trio in the sixth Road picture.
Directed by Hal Walker. Script by Frank Butler, Hal Kanter and William Morrow.
Starring: Bing Crosby, Bob Hope, Dorothy Lamour, Ralph Moody with guest appearances by Bob Crosby, Jane Russell, Dean Martin and Jerry Lewis.

OFF LIMITS (Paramount, 1952)
Another Army comedy also known as Military Policemen.
Directed by George Marshall. Script by Hal Kanter and Jack Sher.
Starring: Bob Hope, Mickey Rooney, Marilyn Maxwell, Carolyn Jones.

SCARED STIFF (Paramount , 1953)
Bob returns to the haunted house he visited in The Ghostbreakers *in a walk-on part.*
Directed by George Marshall. Script by Herbert Baker and Walter de Leon.
Starring: Dean Martin, Jerry Lewis, Lizabeth Scott, Carmen Miranda.

HERE COME THE GIRLS (Paramount, 1953)
Bob as an ageing chorus boy called Stanley Snodgrass.
Directed by Claude Binyon. Script by Edmund Hartmann and Hal Kantor.
Starring: Bob Hope, Tony Martin, Arlene Dahl, Rosemary Clooney.

CASANOVA'S BIG NIGHT (Paramount, 1954)
A historical romp set in Venice with Bob as a tailor's apprentice.
Directed by Norman Z. McLeod. Script by Hal Kantor and Edmund Hartmann.
Starring: Bob Hope, Joan Fontaine, Basil Rathbone, John Carradine.

THE SEVEN LITTLE FOYS (Paramount, 1954)
*True comedy drama about the vaudeville star,
Eddie Foy.*
Directed by Melville Shavelson. Script by
Melville Shavelson and Jack Rose.
Starring: Bob Hope, Milly Vitale, George
Tobias, James Cagney.

CHAIN REACTION (National Playing
Fields Association, 1955)
*Bob appeals for support for the British society
helping sport.*
Directed by David Barclay. Script by Simon
Penrose.
Starring: Bob Hope, Timothy Cooper.

Bob outsinging the "Singing Cowboy", Roy Rogers,
to the evident amusement of Jane Russell in a scene
from *Son of Paleface* (1952).

THAT CERTAIN FEELING (Paramount, 1956)
*Light-hearted romp with Bob playing a
cartoonist.*
Directed by Norman Panama. Script by
Norman Panama, Melvin Frank, I.A.L.
Diamond and William Altman.
Starring: Bob Hope, Eva Maria Saint, George
Sanders, Pearl Bailey, Al Capp.

THE IRON PETTICOAT (British Lion, 1956)
Bob plays an American Air Force officer in Russian-American comedy made in England.
Directed by Ralph Thomas. Script by Ben Hecht.
Starring: Bob Hope, Katharine Hepburn, James Robertson Justice, David Kossoff.

BEAU JAMES (Paramount, 1956)
Comedy about the colourful mayor of New York, Jimmy Walker.
Directed by Melville Shavelson. Script by Jack Rose and Melville Shavelson.
Starring: Bob Hope, Vera Miles, Alexis Smith, Paul Douglas, Jimmy Durante.

THE HEART OF SHOW BUSINESS (Variety Clubs International, 1957)
Bob narrates this account of the organisation's work around the world for the underprivileged.
Directed by Ralph Staub. Script by Jack Rose.
Starring: Bob Hope, Bing Crosby.

PARIS HOLIDAY (United Artists, 1958)
Bob as "Robert Leslie", a movie star who becomes involved in an international farce.
Directed by Gerd Oswald. Script by Edmund Beloin and Dean Riesner, based on an idea by Bob Hope.
Starring: Bob Hope, Fernandel, Martha Hyer, Preston Sturges.

SHOWDOWN AT ULCER GULCH (Saturday Evening Post, 1958)
Bob starred in this "adult Eastern" which promoted the famous American newspaper.
Directed by Shamus Culhane. Script by Simon Simpson.
Starring: Bob Hope, Ernie Kovaks, Edie Adams, Groucho Marx, Chico Marx.

ALIAS JESSIE JAMES (United Artists, 1959)
Bob as a hard-pressed salesman in the Wild West.
Directed by Norman Z. McLeod. Script by William Bowers and Daniel D. Beauchamp.
Starring: Bob Hope, Rhonda Fleming, Wendall Corey, Gary Cooper, Bing Crosby, Roy Rogers.

THE FIVE PENNIES (Paramount, 1959)
Bob guested in this story of jazz musician "Red" Nichols.
Directed by Melville Shavelson. Script by Jack Rose and Melville Shavelson.
Starring: Danny Kaye, Barbara Bel Geddes, Tuesday Weld, Louis Armstrong.

THE FACTS OF LIFE (United Artists, 1960)
A sorely tried businessman trying to cope with domestic life.
Directed by Melvin Frank. Script by Norman Panama and Melvin Frank.
Starring: Bob Hope, Lucille Ball, Ruth Hussey, Don De Fore.

BACHELOR IN PARADISE (MGM, 1961)
Bob plays a writer caught up in the calamitous development of a new housing project.
Directed by Jack Arnold. Script by Valentine Davies and Hal Kanter.
Starring: Bob Hope, Lana Turner, Janis Paige, Jim Hutton.

ROAD TO HONG KONG (United Artists, 1962)
Last of the Road movies with Bob playing a song and dance man.
Directed by Norman Panama. Script by Norman Panama and Melvin Frank.
Starring: Bing Crosby, Bob Hope, Joan Collins, Dorothy Lamour, Robert Morley.

CRITIC'S CHOICE (Warner Bros, 1963)
Bob as a Broadway critic in a sophisticated comedy.
Directed by Don Weis. Script by Jack Sher.
Starring: Bob Hope, Lucille Ball, Marilyn Maxwell, Rip Torn.

CALL ME BWANA (United Artists, 1963)
A writer of books about Africa uses his explorer uncle's diaries for colour.
Directed by Gordon Douglas. Script by Nate Monaster and Johanna Harwood.
Starring: Bob Hope, Anita Ekberg, Edie Adams, Lionel Jeffries.

Caught in the bath! Bob in *Call Me Bwana*, which he filmed in England in 1963.

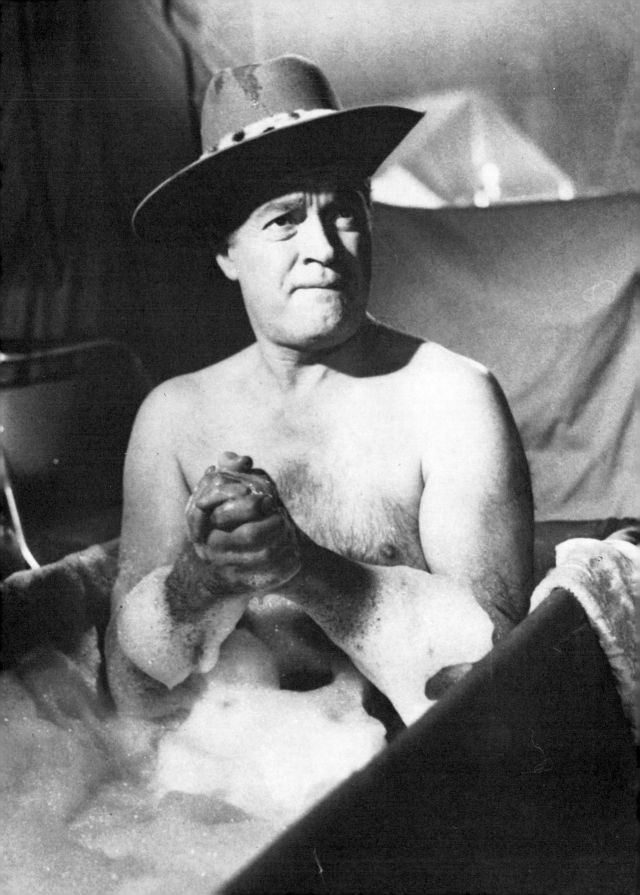

A GLOBAL AFFAIR (MGM, 1963)
Bob as the man in charge of the United Nation's Department of Women's Rights.
Directed by Jack Arnold. Script by Arthur Marx, Bob Fisher and Charles Lederer.
Starring: Bob Hope, Lilo Pulver, Michele Mercier, Elga Anderson.

I'LL TAKE SWEDEN (United Artists, 1965)
Another domestic comedy with Bob as a harassed businessman and father.
Directed by Frederick de Cordova. Script by Nat Perrin, Bob Fisher and Arthur Marx.
Starring: Bob Hope, Tuesday Weld, Dina Merrill, Frankie Avalon.

THE OSCAR (Embassy Pictures, 1965)
Bob played himself as the Master of Ceremonies at the Oscar awards in Hollywood in this melodrama.
Directed by Russell Rouse. Screenplay by Harlan Ellison, Russel Rouse and Clarence Green.
Starring: Stephen Boyd, Eleanor Parker, Milton Berle, Elke Sommer, Joseph Cotten.

NOT WITH MY WIFE, YOU DON'T!
(United Artists, 1966)
A guest appearance in this comedy about infidelity.
Directed by Norman Panama. Script by Norman Panama and Melvin Frank.
Starring: Peter Lawford, Edie Adams, James Dunn.

BOY DID I GET A WRONG NUMBER
(United Artists, 1966)
Bob plays an estate agent who gets involved in a marital mix-up.
Directed by George Marshall. Script by Burt Styler, Albert E. Lewin and George Kennett.
Starring: Bob Hope, Elke Sommer, Phyllis Diller, Cesare Danova.

EIGHT ON THE RUN (United Artists, 1967)
A comedy about a bank clerk left to cope with seven children.
Directed by George Marshall. Script by Albert E. Lewin, Burt Styler, Bob Fisher and Arthur Marx.
Starring: Bob Hope, Phyllis Diller, Jonathan Winters, Jill St. John, and two of Bob's grandchildren, Avis Hope and Robert Hope.

THE PRIVATE ARMY OF SERGEANT O'FARRELL (United Artists, 1968)
A comedy set during World War II with Bob as a master sergeant.
Directed by Frank Tashlin. Script by Frank Tashlin, John L. Greene and Robert M. Fresco.
Starring: Bob Hope, Phyllis Diller, Jeffrey Hunter, Mylene Demongeot.

HOW TO COMMIT MARRIAGE
(Cinerama Releasing, 1969)
Bob in a comedy about the generation gap and modern attitudes towards marriage.
Directed by Norman Panama. Script by Ben Starr and Michael Kanin.
Starring: Bob Hope, Jane Wyman, Jackie Gleason, Tina Louise.

CANCEL MY RESERVATION (United Artists, 1972)
Bob plays a troubled talk-show host who gets involved in a murder case in Arizona.
Directed by Paul Bogart. Screenplay by Louis L'Amour.
Starring: Bob Hope, Eva Maria Saint, Ralph Bellamy, Forrest Tucker.

THE MUPPET MOVIE (Jim Henson Productions, 1979)
A guest appearance for the Peter Pan of movies amidst the comic chaos of the famous puppets.
Directed by James Frawley. Script by Jim Henson.
Starring: Bob Hope and numerous other guest stars.

Game as always — and costumed as outlandishly as ever! Bob co-starring with his golfing partner Jackie Gleason in one of his later movies, *How to Commit Marriage* (1969).